THE SPIRITUAL WISDOM OF SAINT JOHN XXIII

THE SPIRITUAL WISDOM OF
Saint John XXIII

Powerful Insights, Simple Practices,
Heartfelt Prayers

Bill Huebsch

TWENTY
THIRD 23rd
PUBLICATIONS
www.23rdpublications.com

John XXIII, 2004 by John Nava
LOCATION: Corpus Christi University Parish
in Toledo, OH

TWENTY-THIRD PUBLICATIONS

1 Montauk Avenue, Suite 200, New London, CT 06320
(860) 437-3012 ❖ (800) 321-0411 ❖ www.23rdpublications.com

© Copyright 2014 Bill Huebsch. All rights reserved.
No part of this publication may be reproduced in any manner without
prior written permission of the publisher. Write to the Permissions Editor.

ISBN: 978-1-62785-017-9
Library of Congress Catalog Card Number: 2013957103
Printed in the U.S.A.

CONTENTS

INTRODUCTION 1

1 HOLY WATER 5

2 HOLINESS MEANS DYING TO SELF 11

3 HOLY FORGIVENESS:
SEVENTY TIMES SEVEN TIMES 19

4 A HOLY OPEN HEART 25

5 HOLY TRUST IN GOD 33

6 ENOUGH HOLY HUMILITY THAT
ONE CAN LAUGH AT ONESELF 43

7 HOLY POVERTY 53

8 HOLY UNITY IN CHRIST 59

9 HOLY JUSTICE (WITHIN OUR OWN HOUSE) 67

10 HOLY PEACE 73

11 HOLINESS LEADS TO AN OPEN LIFE 81

12 MY BAGS ARE PACKED FOR HOLY DEATH 87

CONCLUSIONS 93

NOTES AND CREDITS 103

INTRODUCTION: A MAN NAMED JOHN

"There once was a man, his name John, sent by God to point out the way to the Life-Light. He came to show everyone where to look, who to believe in. John was not himself the Light; he was there to show the way to the Light." **JOHN 1: 6–8**

This is a personal and intimate story about a man named John: Pope John XXIII. He stood upon the stage of the papacy for a short five years; he was for us like "a flash of heavenly light." The details of his biography and the program of his papacy are important, but as you meet him, what emerges as more important than these is his great heart. The spiritual wisdom of this rather ordinary fellow is rooted in his ability to love and to see love in others. It's connected to his willingness to die to himself over and over again, to risk everything for his faith. He is a saint because, like John the Baptist, he knew his task was to show everyone where to look and whom to believe in. He knew that he himself was not the Light; he was called to help others find their way to the Light.

There is no way to explore his spiritual wisdom without knowing him intimately. As you read this, let him enter into your own heart. Let his presence become real to you, here and now. The purpose of this book is to help you embrace his wisdom, a wisdom that he himself would say came only from God. In a way, this is a prayer book.

The title

I subscribe to a weekly newsmagazine. Each week the cover represents its contents, and there is always one feature that rises above the others in the cover art. But each week as well, the editors share the covers that were in the running but not chosen. On some weeks, I see a second or third cover option, and I think to myself that it would have made the perfect cover.

This book could have had many different titles. I started out calling it *Journey of a Saint,* which I liked because it reflected his own autobiographical *Journey of a Soul.*

My second choice was clever too. I wanted to call it *A Flash of Heavenly Light.* He used this phrase himself in the opening speech of the Council to describe how the idea of calling the Council came to him. The Holy Spirit put the idea into his heart, and he trusted that it was from God.

Later in the writing process, I landed on calling it *The Accidental Saint: John XXIII.* He really did not campaign for this honor. He saw himself as never quite holy enough, always on the journey to greater holiness. He became a saint by accident, not by intention.

One of my advisors suggested this title: *Live, Laugh, Love: the Life of St John XXIII.* This would also have been appropriate because those three actions—living, loving, and laughing—do characterize him very well. They're a big part of this story.

Another candidate for the title was *The Ordinary Saint: John XXIII.* He was indeed an ordinary fellow, and he proves that being ordinary is no obstacle to saintliness. In fact, being your own ordinary self on the journey to holiness is the only way to such sanctity.

Finally, the editors landed on the perfect title: *The Spiritual Wisdom of Saint John XXIII.* The subtitle adds the details: *Powerful Insights, Simple Practices, Heartfelt Prayers.* It turns out that is precisely what this book is. It is a record of Pope John's spiritual wisdom. I pored over his journals, his discourses, his letters, and his other writings. I reread all the encyclicals and conciliar documents. Out of all of these tumbled a framework for holiness, and it is presented here to edify the reader and lead you to greater holiness yourself.

The format

True to the subtitle, each chapter includes powerful insights into Pope John's approach to life, love, and work. When presenting his own words, I often summarized them in order to make them more readable. Each chapter also includes a simple spiritual practice meant for you to use as you are reading. Simply put down the book as each practice comes along and take the time to shift gears and learn about him by experiencing the kind of spiritual practices that he also used. You may wish to keep a short journal of them all.

The spiritual practices are meant to be repeated time and again on your own spiritual journey. I have been doing just that myself. The writing of this book has been my autumn retreat this year. My encounters with Christ, with the Church, and with Pope John himself have been nothing short of life-changing and profound. The spiritual practices presented here have led me more deeply into the heart of the Lord, and I hope they will lead you there too.

The Prayer of Saint John xxiii

Oh God, open our hearts now and renew us
in the spirit of Saint John XXIII.

Take away our fear of this modern world,
as Pope John urged us to do.
Help us befriend all women and men
as our sisters and brothers.
Guide us to be true partners with others
in our modern times
so that science, technology, and medicine
may better serve your purpose and heal your people.

Take away all that divides us,
as Pope John taught us.
May all religions and cultures
come together as one people,
your people, O God of the nations.
Guide us to understand more fully
what the gospel demands of us here today,
and help us be faithful to your law of love.

Take away our judgments and condemnations of others,
as Pope John showed us by example.
Give us hearts filled with tender love
for the poor, the vulnerable, and the rejected.
Guide us to open our wallets as well as our hearts
and share wisely all the produce of the earth
so that no one will starve or suffer because of need.

Chapter 1

HOLY WATER

Angelo Roncalli was born in Sotto il Monte, a small village in Lombardy, which is in northern Italy, on November 25, 1881. As was customary then, he was baptized on the same day by Father Francesco Rebuzzini in the parish church of Santa Maria. He was given the name Angelo Giuseppe. His family encompassed a large collection of siblings and cousins that included neighbors and even occasional strangers, all of whom were seated at the family table each evening. They didn't own their own land but were tenant farmers and gave half the outcome of their farming—milk, veal, and other products—to pay their rent. But their home was filled with simple food and loving people. Angelo's parents, Marianna and Giovanni, had twelve children of their own (three died very young). They lived in a large house with other family members; it was a house in which the cattle and poultry occupied the ground floor. When everyone came together for supper each evening, nearly thirty mouths needed to be fed, not including the livestock. For Angelo, this was his first experience of being in the Church, the "domestic church."

Baptism initiated young Angelo into the Church, but his family raised him in the faith. A shrine to the Madonna stood only a kilometer or so from their farmhouse. The story is told that one day his mother took him and three other siblings to attend a special Mass there. They arrived late and could not find a seat, but his mother lifted the four-year-old Angelo to look through the window. "Look, Angelo," she told him, "see how beautiful the Madonna is." He gazed in through the window at the statue, created with the same dark eyes, broad face, and prominent nose of the Roncallis. But the Virgin Mary was set amid flowers, candlelight, and gold. "I have consecrated you entirely to her," she told him.

Surely this moment seared itself into the young man's understanding of Church. Faith meant beauty, serenity, and love. His mother was continuing for him what his baptism had begun. She was forming him. His father did the same by showing young Angelo how to work, how to love patiently, and how to hold his tongue in charity. He had been baptized on the day of his birth into the universal Church, the local parish, and, above all, the domestic community of faith—and he lived it day in and day out.

In January each year, we celebrate the baptism of Jesus in the River Jordan. The baptism of Jesus initiated him into a community, just as John's had. For Jesus, this meant gathering with his disciples and the women who traveled with him (Luke 8:1–3) and beginning his public ministry. Jesus' baptism is recorded in the gospels of Matthew, Mark, and Luke. John's gospel does not directly describe Jesus' baptism but it does describe John the Baptist's clear proclamation of faith. Here is what we find in the Gospel of John, chapter one:

> John saw Jesus coming toward him and yelled out,
> "Here he is, God's Passover Lamb! He forgives the
> sins of the world! This is the man I've been talking

*about, 'the One who comes after me but is really
ahead of me.' I knew nothing about who he was—
only this: that my task has been to get Israel ready
to recognize him as the God-Revealer. That is why I
came here baptizing with water, giving you a good
bath and scrubbing sins from your life so you can get
a fresh start with God."* JOHN 1:29–31

The scrubbing away of sins was the avenue to holiness that John
XXIII followed from his baptism through the seminary and into
the priesthood. He was attentive to his own sinfulness, which
allowed him to experience the powerful mercy of God all the
more intensely. He knew God's mercy because he experienced
it personally. That experience of God's generous mercy became
a theme of his opening speech at Vatican II.

Late in his life and ministry, Pope John XXIII wrote about
Jesus' baptism, but it almost sounds like he is reflecting on his
own journey of faith. His words form a prayer for us today. Here
is a summary of them.

You were immersed in the River Jordan, O Jesus,
  even though many in the crowd who watched
  did not recognize you.
Tardy faith like this,
  not seeing you for who you really are,
  remains a source of grief for me and many others today.
We want to make you known to the whole world!
  May we receive the grace and power we need
  to press on, speaking of you and demonstrating
    by our lives
    how much you love us.
Since you, who were all loving goodness,

came before John in the river,
we pray that you will draw us likewise to the Jordan:
  to confess our sins and cleanse our souls.
And just as that voice from heaven proclaimed you "chosen,"
  so may we, after living our lives in your name
  and following your pathway,
    hear in our own innermost hearts
    that same divine voice of your Father
    calling us his children.
May this prayer rise from every home
  where people work, love, and suffer.
May the angels gather the prayers of all the children,
  of generous-hearted young men and women,
  of hardworking and self-sacrificing parents,
  and of all who suffer in body and mind
    and present these prayers to God.
From God will flow an abundance of gifts
  and great happiness. Amen.

Pope John is teaching us here that we must embrace our baptism and allow it to be woven into the fabric of our everyday lives, caring for our children, tending the sick, assisting our neighbors, or working to earn our livelihood. Baptism isn't absent from our normal, daily lives but part and parcel of them. We must keep the waters of baptism fresh at all times, conscious that God is giving us gifts through them.

✦Spiritual Exercise

Baptismal Promises

By revisiting our baptismal promises as Pope John XXIII often did, we can get a fresh start in our spiritual lives. All of us pick up baggage along the way: we carry old hurts, memories, losses, and pain. In this spiritual exercise we return to the Jordan, answering the call of the Baptist to set aside these things and go forward with a clean heart.

Step One » *Begin in prayer.*
Ask God to open your heart to his word, which is being spoken to you in the depths of your own heart. Pray that you might hear the divine voice. Pray also for discernment to help you distinguish God's voice from the din of other voices that may be calling you to selfish thoughts and actions.

Step Two » *Pause and become quiet.*
In your mind's eye, imagine you are about to cross a great river without any bridges or boats. What does the river look like to you? How wide and deep is it? What is growing on its banks? Is the bank sandy and shallow or steep and high? Is the water raging by or flowing smoothly and serenely?
Pause here to imagine the river and its banks.

Step Three » *Decide to renew your baptism.*
Standing on one bank looking over to the other, decide that you will walk into the waters, into the current of the river, in order to reach the other side. You know it will be dangerous but you have been promised that on the other bank, your life will be full and happy. It will be a new life.

Before you get your feet wet, think to yourself: what will I leave behind here? What old anger, hatred, or prejudice will I drop? What am I carrying that is too heavy for me? Before I risk my life in these waters, what old patterns of selfishness, hurtfulness, or greed do I have that I should make right? What old failures, bitterness, nights with a lonely heart, or grudges do I want to lay down and let go of forever?

Pause to think back over the months and years of your life. Bring to mind memories of the people, situations, and events that may harbor within them emotions you wish to leave behind. If you feel so inclined, speak with your spiritual director, a confessor, or a friend about this.

Step Four » *Acknowledge your weakness.*

Lay anything down on the river's bank that you do not want to carry. Then step into the water lighter, more confident, and happier than ever before. Wade through these waters, letting them wash away any other dirt that you may have missed. As you make the crossing, promise yourself not to let the things you have left behind become part of your life again. Reject them in your heart.

Then walk up onto the other side as a new person. What is that feeling like? Whom do you join in your new life? Who is there to walk with you and support you? Your journey is not over but you have taken a big step in a new direction.

Step Five » *Hear the voice of God.*

Speak now in your own words to Jesus Christ about this experience. Ask for what you feel you need in order to walk in the new life he has given you through baptism. Open your heart to him as you renew your faith. Hear his voice echoing in the depths of your soul.

Chapter 2

HOLINESS MEANS DYING TO SELF

Pope John XXIII is an accidental saint. He didn't set out in life to become one, and he would be surprised to learn that this honor has been given to him. He always felt he wasn't quite holy enough, not quite living up to his faith, not truly saintly. He was really a very normal, common fellow. His gifts were ones that you or I might possess. His view of the world grew out of being raised by a hardworking but quite average farm family. He did not own fast cars or have a stunning physique. He wasn't one of the world's great artists, he was not a prodigy as a child, and he struggled to keep his weight under control. He sounds like any one of us, doesn't he? And yet, he is a saint. What does this mean in his life and in ours?

Part of the answer to this may come from the great Constitution on the Liturgy at the Second Vatican Council. In that document the Church declared that we are plunged into the paschal mystery. This happens at baptism for us Christians. We go into the water and die to ourselves so that we can come out of the water newly born into love and self-giving.

The Constitution makes reference to St. Paul's teaching on this, which we find in the first five verses of Romans, chapter 6. Here, in part, is what it says there:

> *Didn't you realize we packed up and left [our old way of living] for good? That is what happened in baptism. When we went under the water, we left the old country of sin behind; when we came up out of the water, we entered into the new country of grace— a new life in a new land!*
>
> *That's what baptism into the life of Jesus means. When we are lowered into the water, it is like the burial of Jesus; when we are raised up out of the water, it is like the resurrection of Jesus. Each of us is raised into a light-filled world by our Father so that we can see where we're going in our new grace-sovereign country.*

This means that we are immersed in the life and death and resurrection of Jesus Christ. We are intimately connected to him. This teaching in article six reminds us that we are all called to die to ourselves out of love for others and God. Such dying to self is not very popular today, but it was the hallmark of Pope John XXIII's life and ministry. Self-giving love is what leads to holiness, according to Pope John and also article 42 of the Constitution on the Church. Love is the pathway. Learning how to imitate Christ means learning to forgive, be generous, and love others recklessly.

Later in the Council, the Constitution on the Church in the Modern World described the dignity of the human person by proclaiming that the mystery of humanity becomes clear only in light of the paschal mystery. In article 22 of this constitution, the bishops wrote that Christ has opened up a pathway for us to follow. This pathway is that of dying to self, enduring the uncertainty of the grave, experiencing the joy of new life, and responding to this by loving recklessly. "If we follow this path, life and death are made holy and acquire a new meaning," they wrote. "All this holds true not only for Christians but also for all people of good will in whose hearts grace is active invisibly." In other words, the pathway to holiness they outlined is not meant only for Christians, but for all people. Everyone is called to die to himself or herself. Our human dignity depends on it. We're all called to love our enemies and do good to those who hate us. We're all called to be last, all called to take up our crosses, and all called to sacrifice ourselves for the good of others.

Following this pathway is what led Pope John to sainthood. Indeed, for him and for us, there is no pathway other than the journey that requires that we carry our cross joyfully, die to ourselves willingly, and learn well the art of self-giving love. This is the secret of holiness; it is the secret of Pope John's life.

Father Angelo Roncalli spoke of this in an address in 1907 at the seminary in his home diocese of Bergamo. He was just two years ordained at the time. In the address, he describes for us the connection between the paschal mystery and the journey to sainthood. As we read it now, more than one hundred years later, his voice is prophetic, describing what would become the pathway of his own life. Here is a summary of that speech.

There is a tendency to make saints
    into larger figures than they really are.
We pluck them out of their historical settings
      and cultural milieus

and weave legends about them,
focusing very strongly on what great human achievement
they had
while ignoring, perhaps a little too much,
the work of grace in their lives.
After all, what is a saint anyway?
Sometimes we make them into characters
that fit better into a work of fiction
than into the real world in which we all live.
To be a saint is to practice self-giving love at all times;
it is to make oneself second in line, not first;
it is to suppress the desire to make a big show of things,
to put aside the ways in which people might praise you,
and to tend the flame of love for God.
A saint keeps his or her focus on loving God,
but also on loving one's fellow men and women.
A saint trusts that God speaks in our depths,
teaching us a law that we do not make for ourselves
but which comes from the divine heart:
the law of love.
This surpasses all the fragile accomplishments of the world
and directs us on our true pathway to holiness.

Pope John is teaching us here that the pathway to sainthood or
to holiness is traveled by common men and women in their daily
lives when they practice the art of self-giving love. When we allow
the grace of the paschal mystery to direct us toward the teachings of our master, Jesus Christ, it is not complicated. It doesn't
require complex theology. We simply and faithfully imitate the
self-emptying, generous, and unconditional love of Christ.
For Pope John and for us, the chief tool that keeps us on this
journey of faith is prayer. He used a form of reflective prayer that

has roots in Ignatian spirituality. This form of prayer is called the *Examen*. In it, we pause and look back over our shoulders at the day just ending. We search around in that day for signs of God's presence and gifts, but we also find our own selfishness, failures, and disappointments. Using the *Examen* keeps us centered on the road to holiness. It helps us examine the people, events, and situations of each day in order to make corrections for tomorrow or to be filled with gratitude for God's gifts of today—and both are true every day.

Spiritual Exercise

THE DAILY EXAMEN

[Adapted from an unknown Ignatian source]

St. Ignatius believed that the daily *Examen* was one of the prayers that should be mandatory for all his followers. It leads to prayer-filled mindfulness, and Pope John used it throughout his life. Memorize these steps and use this exercise every day.

As you prepare to enter into this daily exercise, find that place in your life where you can sit quietly for at least fifteen minutes. Turn off the TV and media, including your mobile phone. Use these notes slowly and confidently. God is about to provide you with a profound experience of divine love. Begin with these words of Scripture:

> *The word is right here and now—as near as the tongue in your mouth, as near as the heart in your chest. Look at what I've done for you today: I've placed in front of you life and goodness, death and evil. Choose life so that you and your children will*

> *live. And love God, your God, listening obediently to him, firmly embracing him.*
> **DEUTERONOMY 30:14, 15, 19**

Step One ⟫ *Recall that you are in the presence of God.*
No matter where you are—hilltop or valley, country or city, in a crowd or alone—you are a creature in the midst of creation. As you quiet yourself, become aware that God is present within you, in the creation that surrounds you, in your body, and in those around you.

Pause now briefly here to allow the presence of God to well up around you. Let it fill your heart with light and peace.

Step Two ⟫ *Call on the Spirit.*
The Creator, who brought you forth into being, is concerned for you. The Spirit of God, sent by Christ, will remind you that you are gifted to help bring creation to its fullness. Ask the Holy Spirit to let you look on all you see with love.

> *Love never gives up. Love cares more for others than for self. Love doesn't want what it doesn't have. Love doesn't strut, doesn't have a swelled head, and doesn't force itself on others. Love isn't always "me first," doesn't fly off the handle, doesn't keep score of the sins of others, doesn't revel when others grovel. Love takes pleasure in the flowering of truth, puts up with anything, trusts God always, always looks for the best, never looks back, but keeps going to the end.*
> **1 CORINTHIANS 13:4–7**

Turn your heart toward the Spirit of God. Ask the Spirit to give you the "eyes of love."

Step Three » *Look back over your shoulder.*
Spend a moment looking over your day with gratitude for this day's gifts. This is the longest of the steps. Recall the events of your day; explore the context of your actions. Search for the internal movements of your heart and your interaction with what was before you. Ask what you were involved in and who you were with, and review your hopes and hesitations.

Let your heart search for meaningful moments and events in your day. You are, at the same moment, rummaging around in your memories for the presence of God.

Allow God to speak, challenge, encourage, and teach you. Thus you will come to know that Christ is with you. Christ will continually invite you to love your neighbor as yourself and will strengthen you to do this.

Be concrete and let special moments or pleasures spring to mind. Recall the smell of your morning coffee, the taste of something good that you ate, the laugh of a child, the fragrance of a flower, the smile brought forth by a kind word, a lesson that you learned. Take stock of what you received and what you gave. Give thanks to God for favors received.

Also look at your permanent gifts that allow your participation in this day. Recall your particular strengths in times of difficulty, your ability to hope in times of weakness, your sense of humor and your life of faith, your intelligence and health, your family and friends. God the Father gives you these to draw you into the fullness of life. As you move through the details of your day, give thanks to God for God's presence in the big and the small things of your life.

Pause to think back over your day, hour by hour, moment by moment, bringing back to mind how your day unfolded.

Step Four » *Be grateful.*

Let your heart gradually fill with thankfulness for the gifts you have been given. Ask God to free you from envying others for their gifts and to become grateful for your own.

Ask God to send you the Holy Spirit to help you look at your actions and attitudes and motives with honesty and patience. "But when the Friend comes, the Spirit of the Truth, he will take you by the hand and guide you into all the truth there is" (John 16:13). The Holy Spirit inspires you to see with growing freedom the development of your life story. The Spirit gives a freedom to look upon yourself without condemnation and without complacency and thus be open to growth.

Ask that you will learn and grow as you reflect, thus deepening your knowledge of self and your relationship with God.

Step Five » *Prayer.*

The final step is to speak heart-to-heart with Jesus and, with him, look forward to tomorrow. Here you speak with Jesus about your day. You share your thoughts on your actions, attitudes, feelings, and interactions. Perhaps during this time you may feel led to seek forgiveness, ask for direction, share a concern, express gratitude, and so forth. Open yourself to his guidance and presence for the rest of this day and tomorrow.

Having reviewed this day of your life, look upon yourself with compassion and see your need for God and try to realize God's manifestations of concern for you. Express sorrow for sin—the obscuring darkness that surrounds us all—and especially ask forgiveness for the times you resisted God's light today. Give thanks for grace—the enlightening presence of God—and especially praise God for the times you responded in ways that allowed you to better see God's life. Resolve with Jesus to move forward in action where appropriate.

Chapter 3

HOLY FORGIVENESS:
SEVENTY TIMES
SEVEN TIMES

P ope John seemed to find it most difficult to love
when people spoke ill of him, or when they caused
him suffering of one kind or another. And who
wouldn't find love difficult then? What makes him
saintly is that he sought, not always perfectly, I'm
sure, to work through this and come out in the light.

For the Christian, it seems to go without saying that our main
task is to follow the teachings of our master, Jesus Christ, and
live in love. I say this seems to make sense because what often
happens instead is that we throw up a dust cloud of religious
ideas that make love seem unreachable. We busy ourselves with
theology and a long history of church politics, and sometimes
this can occupy us so thoroughly that we forget our main mission, which as I said above, is to live in love.

When Jesus was asked about this, his answer came back very
clearly. It didn't have much to do with ecclesial policy, dogmatic

belief systems, or even rubrics and rituals. It was much simpler:

> *"I've told you these things for a purpose: that my joy*
> *might be your joy, and your joy wholly mature. This*
> *is my command: Love one another the way I loved*
> *you. This is the very best way to love. Put your life*
> *on the line for your friends. You are my friends when*
> *you do the things I command you. I'm no longer call-*
> *ing you servants because servants don't understand*
> *what their master is thinking and planning. No, I've*
> *named you friends because I've let you in on every-*
> *thing I've heard from the Father."* JOHN 15:11–15

Pope John XXIII was often hurt by the criticisms or ridicule of others. He was not considered an "A-list" priest, bishop, or cardinal. He spent much of his adult life living far away from Rome and all the "A-list" church insiders who lived and worked there. He was almost always something of an outsider and was truly surprised when he was given an honor of any kind.

He often wrote in his journal about being hurt by others. Here is a summary of one such entry.

One of the examples of faith used by St. Francis de Sales,
    which I often remember and ponder, is:
    "I am like a bird singing in a thicket of thorns."
I want to keep this very much in my conscious thoughts
    as I go about each day of my life.

When something has hurt my feelings,
    I must say very little to anyone.
I must carefully cultivate the ability to withhold judgment
    either of people or situations

that cause me to suffer a little.
In fact, I must pray for those who hurt me,
    showing endless patience and kindness toward them.
Any other way of reacting to being hurt
    is not loving
    and is, therefore, not in line with the teachings of Jesus
    nor of spiritual growth.
Charity must prevail at all costs!

Charity, indeed. And Pope John felt blessed to have the right personality and temperament for this. In 1948 he wrote:

I am inclined in my own personality
    toward seeing the good in everyone.
I am not inclined to criticize others
    or to look down on them
    or to judge them harshly.
As I grow older and more mature,
    I seem to be out of touch
    with many of the younger clerics with whom I work.
They tend to show distrust and a lack of courtesy
    to the humble, poor, and socially inferior.
This breaks my heart to see!

Pope John is teaching us here that being loving sometimes means simply biting our tongues and zipping our lip, even when we are wronged. Dying to self sometimes means "being the big one" and letting go of small hurts and offenses. This seems to be the meaning of that mysterious text in Matthew 5:38–42 where Jesus teaches:

"Here's another old saying that deserves a second

look: 'Eye for eye, tooth for tooth.' Is that going to
get us anywhere? Here's what I propose: 'Don't hit
back at all.' If someone strikes you, stand there and
take it. If someone drags you into court and sues for
the shirt off your back, giftwrap your best coat and
make a present of it. And if someone takes unfair
advantage of you, use the occasion to practice
the servant life. No more tit-for-tat stuff. Live
generously."

Doesn't that sound like what Pope John was saying in his journal just above? This is a difficult teaching to really live by, but Pope John helps us see that it is possible. In Matthew, chapter 5, verse 48, Jesus sums this up, and I can hear these words on the lips of Pope John: "In a word, what I'm saying is, *Grow up.* You're kingdom subjects. Now live like it. Live out your God-created identity. Live generously and graciously toward others, the way God lives toward you."

Later in his life, Pope John elaborated on this thought. He warned us to beware of misunderstandings when they arise. We need not come to blows because of them, he said. We should be careful not to exaggerate them or allow them to come between us. In summary, he added:

We should be the first to explain away such
  misunderstandings,
    and to put things right once more between
    ourselves and others.
We should avoid feeling resentment about them.

Disagreements arise even among people of good will,
  and this is natural;

it does no harm to peace and harmony
as long as we are careful to control them.
In fact, the Lord may even make use of such misunderstandings.
Grace is always able to overcome them
and clear them away.
We should always recall the words of the Lord
that surprised the world when he said them,
that there is more joy and peace of heart
when we die to ourselves
than when we demand that we are always
in the right.

Spiritual Exercise

FORGIVE SEVENTY TIMES SEVEN TIMES

It's easy for us to remember the people we hate or with whom we are angry. We keep a short list in our minds of those who have hurt us, insulted us, or caused us suffering. Sometimes we even harbor a secret resentment that contains within it a plan to "get back at them" in order to balance the scales, even though we know there will be no joy in doing that. In this exercise we will become conscious of these feelings and become willing to offer them to Christ in prayer.

Step One » *Begin in prayer.*
Ask God to open your heart to his word, which is being spoken to you in the depths of your own heart. Pray that you might hear the divine voice. Pray also for discernment to help you distinguish God's voice from the din of other voices that may

be calling you to selfish thoughts and actions.

Step Two » *Take stock.*

Using something on which to write (a tablet, paper pad, or even the back of an old envelope), think back over the past couple of weeks. Record the names of people whom you have encountered who still linger in your mind with an "unsettled account" with you. Think about people you have criticized for one thing or another. Or think of people whom you consider "stupid" or "ignorant" about things. These are likely people whom you have not yet forgiven. Bring to mind those whom you judge to be socially inferior to you and your entourage.

Pause here to make your list.

Step Three » *Speak with Christ.*

Once you have your little list, take it to prayer with you. Ask the Lord to send his Spirit to give you a new heart about each of them. Name each one and hold them before you as you pray. You don't have to actually start liking them or spending time with them as friends, but you do need to allow your heart to swell with self-emptying love for them. The real challenge is to begin to see what gifts they may have actually brought into your life. This is how you will become a saint like Pope John.

Pause here to move toward prayer.

Invite Christ to send his Spirit into your heart to heal you and give you a fresh beginning. Open your heart to his grace and power; it will be enough for you.

Chapter 4

A HOLY OPEN HEART

Before he was elected to the papacy, Pope John served in several key positions in the Church. He served the churches of Bulgaria, Turkey, Greece, France, and Venice before his final move to Rome in 1958. During this time he developed an attitude and language of openness toward non-Catholics. He saw all men and women as his concern and never failed to be gently inclusive in his address to the people.

This feature of his life contributed greatly to the spirit he brought to the papacy and especially to Vatican II. There the bishops of the world drew from his spirit a sense of concern for the entire human family. In fact, the first official statement of the Council was addressed, not to Catholics, but to all men and women of the world.

> We wish to convey to all people and to all nations the message of salvation, love, and peace which we have received from Jesus Christ, the bishops said (summarized here). In fact that is the very reason we have gathered

here in Rome for this Council. We want to renew our own inner life, the bishops said, and we want to offer all people of our time the chance to hear the powerful message of love and peace proclaimed in the Gospels. Even though we are part of the Church, we aren't strangers to the concerns of today's people, people all over the world. We are open to them, the bishops wrote. We think of them as sisters and brothers.

United here from every nation on earth we are keenly aware of people's anxieties, their sorrows and desires and hopes, especially those who are poor and weak or suffering from hunger, misery, or ignorance. We want to help the world end war; this is our greatest wish. We proclaim that all men and women are sisters and brothers no matter what race, nation, or faith to which they belong. We also want to see social justice become a reality. We invite everyone on earth to share in this great endeavor.

This new spirit of partnership with the world replaced a pre-Pope John idea that the world is the enemy of the Church. The language of Vatican II showed a remarkably new attitude toward the world and other faiths. The bishops at the Council used words such as "sister and brother churches" to describe Protestants who had once been called heretics and schismatics. They spoke eloquently of cooperation and collaboration with others. There was wide use of the word "freedom" within the Council texts, and the Church was called a pilgrim. This new openness to others is now enshrined in the Church forever because of Vatican II, which became for us "a new Pentecost."

Surely the bishops at the Council drew their inspiration

from the leader: Pope John XXIII. In his farewell remarks to
the Bulgarian people in November 1934, Angelo Roncalli expressed this wonderful, holy openness. He said, in summary:

There is a wonderful old tradition in Ireland
    that I like very much.
On Christmas Eve, every house
    sets a light in the window.
Its purpose is to let Jesus and Mary know,
    just in case they are passing by on that night
    looking for an inn,
        that there is a family in this house
        that would welcome them with open arms.
There is a fire to warm them
    and a table around which to share a meal.

No one knows the ways of the future!
    No matter where I go in the world as I leave here,
    if someone from Bulgaria passes by my house
    you will find a lamp in the window,
        lit just for you.
Knock! Please, knock!
    I will not ask you if you are a Catholic or not;
    it is enough that you are my friend from Bulgaria: enter!
Two brotherly arms will embrace you;
    the warm heart of a friend will welcome you.
For such is the Christian charity of the Lord,
    the expression of which has sweetened my life.

Pope John is teaching us here that God loves all men and wom-
en, regardless of what church to which they belong. We are all
children of the one God. Therefore, let us take each other in

with generous hearts and open arms.

Later in his life as he was dying, Pope John once again returned to this theme. He seemed to sense an urgency that is driving us toward one another as friends, not away from each other as enemies and combatants. On his journey to sainthood, Pope John allowed his heart to grow open to others. Such openness is a hallmark of holiness because it requires us to trust in Divine Providence to control all things and lead us to peace with one another. Here is what Pope John said, in summary form:

More than ever before in history
    we are called today
    to serve all men and women
        and not merely other Catholics.
We must vigorously defend the rights
    of every human person on earth,
    and not merely the rights of the Catholic Church.
In the last fifty years—years of war and terrible violence—
    we have come to understand this more clearly,
    as I said in my opening speech at the Council.
It isn't so much that the gospel has changed
    but that we are finally beginning to understand it better.
I am an old man now and have seen
        great changes in my lifetime.
    I lived twenty years in the East and eight in France.
I have compared cultures and traditions;
    I have met many men and women who are different
        from me.
I have come to understand from all this
    that the moment has come to discern the signs of the times
    and to seize the opportunity for dialogue and partnership
    that will take us forward into a future without fear.

The Church of the early 1960s was one in which there were those who called for rapid and extensive reform in the liturgy, the place of lay people, the role of bishops in Church authority, and the Church's place in society. And there were also others who believed such reforms were not needed. These latter believed that what was needed was a stronger assertion of Church authority in the face of certain modern movements of thought.

But in a Church that was often agitated by these two currents, one of the progressives and the other of the traditionalists, Pope John surprised both, recalling them to considerations above and beyond their opinions, to a sphere where such opinions no longer matter. His dismay was due to his conviction that Christianity had not yet understood all the requirements of the gospel.

Monsignor Guerry, the Archbishop of Cambrai, gives us an insight into this feature of Pope John's leadership. In a private conversation, the pope confided to the monsignor his grief that so many people of good will in the world thought that the Church rejected and condemned them, that it no longer loved them. Then, showing Monsignor Guerry the crucifix that always stood on his table, Pope John said with emotion: "But I must be like Christ. I open wide my arms to embrace them. I love them, and I am their father. I am always ready to welcome them." Then, turning to him again, he said: "Monsignor, all that the gospel requires of us has not yet been understood."

Pope John is asking us here to open our own hearts, to allow the good of humankind, and not only our own good, to dominate in our thinking. These are the reflections of a saint, a man who allowed the Spirit to change him.

OPENING THE DOORS OF OUR HEARTS

Modern life is packed with noise. We have to turn off the TVs, mobile phones, tablets, and junk mail in order to become conscious of what is immediately around us. We often see people but actually "overlook them," looking right past them at the next stimulus that comes along. This exercise will help us become conscious of those toward whom God is calling us to open our hearts.

Step One » *Begin in prayer.*
Find a place where you can comfortably sit for a few minutes of quiet time. Turn off your mobile phone and television. Ask God to open your heart to his word, which is being spoken to you in the depths of your own heart. Pray that you might hear the divine voice. Pray also for discernment to help you distinguish God's voice from the din of other voices that may be calling you to selfish thoughts and actions.

Step Two » *Take stock.*
In your mind's eye, imagine a long, endless wall standing in front of you. Imagine that it has a single doorway. The door is shut. Behind it are the people of good will of whom you are unaware. They may be people whom you tend to shun, ignore, or reject. In this exercise, don't turn your mind to murderers, pirates, or hijackers. Turn it toward people of good will, people who seek to do the best they can, people who are simply different from you. Who are these people? Who has become invisible to you?

Is it the many old people in nursing homes who have no one to visit them? Is it the frightened moms and dads who are immigrants, hiding for fear someone may discover them? Is it the people of nations where chronic poverty is the rule of life? Think about people within your own nation who have no homes, those unwashed faces you see on street corners or under bridges. Think about people who profess a faith you do not hold yourself, perhaps a faith you do not fully understand. Think about people who have, by no intention of their own, lived in the pathway of war or natural disasters. Think also about those whom you judge to be morally inferior to yourself.

Pause to begin bringing these people to mind. When you have made a good beginning, go to the next step.

Step Three ❯ *Your side of the wall.*
Now turn your mind to that group of people whom you would imagine to be on your side of the door. Who are they? Are they from your own nation, your own religion, your own race, culture, or marital status? Are they from your particular political party? From your age group? Your family?

Step Four ❯ *Reconsider.*
Pause to consider these two groups: the one on your side of the door and the one on the other side of the door. See them there in your mind's eye. Hear now again the words of Pope John:

More than ever before in history
   we are called today
     to serve all men and women
        and not merely other Catholics.
We must vigorously defend the rights of every human person
   on earth,
        and not merely the rights of the Catholic Church.

And again, from Pope John:

Two brotherly arms will embrace you;
    the warm heart of a friend will welcome you.
For such is the Christian charity of the Lord,
    the expression of which has sweetened my life.

Step Five » *Prayer.*

Now turn your heart to Jesus Christ in prayer. Invite him to visit you today and walk with you. Offer him your work, encounters, quiet times, and play times today. Be open to his grace, which is offered to you continually; it is enough for you.

Chapter 5

HOLY TRUST IN GOD

God, we believe, speaks to us in prayer. John XXIII's journals and other writings show that he believed this with all his heart. He made it his goal to become increasingly a person of "intense" prayer. He wanted each day to be one long prayer; indeed, he lived and breathed his prayer.

We know he prayed the traditional prayers of the Church: the Mass, the Liturgy of the Hours (called during his life the "Divine Office"), the Spiritual Exercises of St. Ignatius, and the devotions of the Church. But he also prayed in other ways. He wrote many personal prayers and shared them with others in his deeply intimate, very personal way. He seemed to embody what St. Paul says in Philippians 4:11–13:

> *Actually, I don't have a sense of needing anything personally. I've learned by now to be quite content whatever my circumstances. I'm just as happy with little as with much, with much as with little. I've found the recipe for being happy whether full or hungry, hands full or hands empty. Whatever I have, wherever I am, I can make it through anything in the One who makes me who I am.*

For example, as a very young man, Angelo Roncalli wrote this prayer, which is found in his journal. Here is a summary.

O Jesus, you are full of mercy;
     give your grace to me, I pray.
May your grace be with me;
     may it give me strength,
     and may it stay with me to the end of my life.
Help me to desire only what you desire for me,
     what is most dear to your divine heart.
May whatever I want also be exactly what you want for me;
     help me to desire only that.
     Help me likewise to reject and hate
          what you also hate.
Imitating your son, let me die to myself,
     let me die to all that is not of you
          even if that means being rejected during my lifetime.
Above all, O Jesus, plant within me the desire
     to rest only in you
     and find my peace only in you.
You are the true source of all peace
     and every heart finds rest only in you;
          indeed, apart from you everything is restless.
I long, therefore, to live always near your great heart. Amen.

Such prayers show how deeply prayerful Pope John XXIII was and how this prayerfulness was basic to his vision of Church, other people, and the Council itself.

Pope John also listened to God in prayer. He knew that God often speaks in the core of us, nudging us and sending us intuitions inspired by the Holy Spirit. The council he launched would teach this explicitly. Deep within us, we read in article 16 of the great Constitution on the Church in the Modern World (and summarized here), we detect a law that we have not laid upon ourselves but which we must obey. Calling us to love and to do what is good and avoid evil, the voice of conscience sounds in our hearts at the right moments of life. For we have in our hearts a law inscribed by God. Our conscience is our most secret core and our sanctuary; there we are alone with God, whose voice echoes in our depths.

On being elected pope, John was very conscious that he had a rare opportunity to assist the peoples of the world to live together in peace and to advance the cause of the gospels. He strongly desired that his pontificate be one known for compassion and the open arms of Christ to the world, on which he meditated daily.

The idea of calling a council, only the twenty-first such gathering in the nearly 2000-year history of the Christian church, therefore, seemed to him to be that program of work that would meet his desires. But the idea did not arise in him without proper discernment and development. It was not a "private revelation" that came to him.

For many years in Rome, since the beginning of the reign of Pope Pius XII, there had been talk of a Council. Early in his own pontificate, Pope John had talked about it with a few close advisors. Some were in favor, others opposed. John kept the idea top secret for several months, speaking only to those who could help him be certain the council was of God and not an ego trip of his own. He wished to submit to the Lord's will and to be of great care in discernment.

He had learned to test ideas that came to him in prayer, but when they were tested and found to be of God, he also learned to trust them and to organize his life around them. He knew self-deception was possible, even for the pope, and was careful not to allow that to interfere. He evaluated new ideas according to how much they "stuck" in his mind and heart. He tried to discern the inner sense of rightness and peace they produced. In this way, he was well-practiced in the Ignatian school of the Spiritual Exercises.

One wonderful example of this came in his opening speech at the Council. In it he surprised the world by sharing about how the idea for a council had arisen in his mind. Here is that portion of his opening speech in summary form:

Let me tell you
   for the sake of the historical record
   about how the idea for a council
      came suddenly to mind for me.
The words "an ecumenical council"
   came to my lips for the first time
   in the presence of the cardinals of the Church
   on January 25, 1959,
      on the Feast of St. Paul
      at the basilica dedicated to his name.
This idea was completely unexpected,
   "like a flash of heavenly light."

Like a flash of heavenly light. John had a deep sense that God was leading him to do this work, but he did not employ any feasibility studies, planning committees, or consultants. Instead, he listened in an Ignatian fashion for the sense of rightness within himself. He allowed the idea to linger within his imagination, testing it this way and that. And once he knew it was right, he went forward with vigor even in the face of opposition and downright sabotage from his own team. He spoke of these naysayers in his opening speech, as though to put to rest what he considered their failure to see that God is leading us. Here is what he said, in summary form:

As I go about my pastoral work each day,
  I sometimes must listen to people who,
  though filled with enthusiasm for the Church,
    don't have any sense of judgment.
They believe that these modern times
  will see the ruin of the Church.
  They believe that this age is somehow worse
    than past ages.
But they have obviously learned nothing from history,
  and history is the "teacher of life."
These people think that in past ages
  everything was perfect!
  They forget that it was not!
  It never is.
I feel I must disagree with these "prophets of gloom"
  who are always speaking as though
  a disaster will overtake us,
    as though it's the end of the world!
Actually, in our day as in past ones,
  God is leading us to a new way of living together
  in the human family.
We are optimistic that God is directing us
  where God wants us to go
  and this is good!
We cannot know for sure what God wants for us,
  and yet everything, even our disagreements,
  will lead to the growth of the Church.

Pope John is teaching us to listen carefully to our own intuitions and to test them to be sure they are of God. Then, once these intuitions are trusted, he is teaching us to move forward on the strength of the certainly that God is with us. For Pope John, the idea of a council, that "flash of heavenly light," came to him in answer to prayer.

Prayer is often called a "dialogue" between God and us. But, in prayer, while we usually speak words toward God, whether oral or silent, God does not, ordinarily, speak words back to us. God, Pope John knew, "speaks" not many words to us, but rather a single word. The word divinely spoken is nothing less than the life of the one who prays. For we are aware that God is with us: continually creating us, constantly loving us, and revealing us to ourselves and to one another at all times.

We are spoken. We are the ones who are spoken in prayer, and to enter into our lives as divine in their source and divine in their destiny is to enter into prayer. We are bound up with God in such a dramatic way that the intricacies of our lives are filled with divine energy. So hearing God is hearing our lives as they are drawn into God in the everydayness with which we live. Pope John's journal is teeming with entries that echo this.

Spiritual Exercise

LEARNING TO LISTEN IN PRAYER

Step One » *Begin in prayer.*
Ask God to open your heart to his word, which is being spoken to you in the depths of your own heart. Pray that you might hear the divine voice. Pray also for discernment to help you distinguish God's voice from the din of other voices that may be calling you to selfish thoughts and actions.

How can we learn to hear? How can we learn to offer our full selves in prayer?

Step Two » *Become comfortable and quiet.*
Whether you are sitting, walking, driving, kneeling, working in the garden, or folding the laundry, let your mind become quiet. This sort of prayer isn't something that will necessarily occur in a chapel or at formal prayer. The sense of the Spirit with which we are blessed in this prayer of listening isn't very easily scheduled.

Step Three » *Pause deeply and allow yourself to relax and rest.*
Drop your shoulders and relax your clenched jaw. Settle your mind. The idea isn't that we must learn some complex system of exercises that will guarantee success here. It's rather that each one of us learns to relax as we are able. This relaxing is more like putting a car into "neutral" than like shifting gears into "park." Take just a moment to quiet yourself and become ready to pray.

Step Four » *Bring to mind that for which you wish to pray.*
Pope John was concerned that the Church seemed out of touch with the modern world. He wanted it to penetrate more deeply the consciousness of men and women of good will throughout the world. But for us, what comes to mind may be
    a friend soon to visit,
    someone you have wronged,
    a challenging moment,
    a want or need,
    a night dream or a daydream,
    your own sense of well-being,
    a problem to solve,
    or a new insight.
You won't have to work very hard at this because what we have

to pray for is already there, waiting in our deep minds to be awakened by this simple way of paying attention to it. Bring to mind gently whatever is there; let it come slowly, willingly, and let it linger in the shadows of your consciousness, almost at the back of your mind. If someone were to ask you, "What's on your mind these days?" that would be your "agenda" for prayer. You may wish to mix this "agenda" with Scripture, spiritual reading, or a reflection on the mysteries of our faith.

Let these concerns and thoughts come to mind spontaneously for you.

Step Five ❯❯ *Watch and listen to what you see and hear.*
Pay attention to your own feelings, ideas, and imagination. Be present to God, the Sacred One. If you sense resistance, check that, for in it you will find what blocks you. If you sense consolation, that deep sense of rightness and well-being, you are very close to the heart of the Lord.

This is the most important part of this prayer. Seek to hear how God is directing you; know that the divine direction is always to love and never to hate.

Step Six ❯❯ *Become conscious of what you hear and see.*
Begin to consolidate your thinking and mentally record your experience. Try putting words on it, letting it gel, and even writing down a few thoughts. From time to time, you may want to share what you have heard with others, especially when discerning or praying about extremely significant or terribly difficult matters. This is precisely what Pope John was doing that day at St. Paul's church when he spoke to the cardinals.

Step Seven ❯❯ *Become grateful.*
Let gratitude well up within you; be thankful for the gifts you

have received, and know them to have God as their source. Bask in gratitude for a moment, not coming away from your prayer until you are ready. Let your heart swell with praise—the kind of wordless, speechless awe you feel in the face of beauty, love, and generosity. For you have just seen beauty, love, and endless divine generosity. You have just experienced your own "flash of heavenly light" as God spoke to you in prayer.

Step Eight » *Speak to Christ in your own words now.*
If words do not come, be present to Christ without words. Let the presence of the Holy One sweep into your heart and fill you. You will experience being filled with light!

The outcomes are clear. By this method of letting the Divine One enter into the "stuff" of our ordinary lives, we are drawn into God more and more. We feel God's acceptance, God's unconditional forgiveness, God's urgent call to us to live as we are created to. And in this, we will be converted into ever-deeper relationship with God; and this will lead us to lives of service, honesty, love, and witness. The everyday details of our lives are touched by Divine Presence, and we come to experience that same "flash of heavenly light" that Pope John did: the voice of God echoing in our souls.

Chapter 6

ENOUGH HOLY HUMILITY THAT ONE CAN LAUGH AT ONESELF

S hortly after he assumed his regular day-to-day activities in the Vatican, Pope John invited a newly appointed archbishop to have supper with him. During the meal, the archbishop complained to Pope John that the burdens of being a busy archbishop were keeping him from sleeping well. Pope John said in reply:

I'm sorry to hear that, Archbishop.
    The same thing happened to me
    immediately after I become pope.
But then my guardian angel appeared to me in a daydream
    and said to me: "John, don't take yourself so seriously."
Ever since then I sleep soundly every night!

This ability to see himself as he really was, and the humility to laugh at himself, were characteristics of Pope John's journey to holiness. Indeed, such humor is a sure sign of holiness; it's a gift given by God to us. In the case of Pope John, it allowed him to look past the overly zealous protocol of the Vatican and see the real person he was. He often joked about his own weight, about the Roncalli physique, and about his foibles and faults. Shouldn't we all do that? Isn't the ability to see ourselves as we really are, admit what we see, and find humor in it all, a sign that we know God loves us and laughs right along with us?

If we laugh at ourselves, after all, we gain great personal freedom. No one else can hurt us, because we've already come to know our own shortcomings and oddities. We are free of the fear of what others may say about us, free to laugh and have a little fun in life. How, Pope John might have wondered, did religion get to be so grim? After all, it's the good news we offer people, not the bad news!

As he was moving into his apartment in the Vatican, Pope John was wandering around the various rooms, getting to know his new surroundings. In one of the rooms, some delivery men were bringing in boxes and crates of his books and belongings. Seeing them, Pope John asked, "Am I disturbing you, my sons?" One of the delivery men, who could not see it was John but thought it was a coworker making a joke, replied, "After you stop playing the fool, come over here and give me a hand." Once he realized it was the pope, of course, he was embarrassed. So to put him at ease, Pope John said to him, "You and I belong to the same party."

"But I don't belong to any party," the worker said.

"Look at the width of my frame," said the pope. "For people like you and me, membership in the party of the stoutly built is a foregone conclusion." Such personal freedom to laugh at ourselves comes only when we give up the idea that we must be anything other than what God makes us to be.

Pope John paid serious attention to all the challenges that faced him as pope. He knew he held a central and key leadership role in the Church. He gave his closest attention to every task or request, no matter how small. More than ever before in his life, Pope John keenly felt responsible for leading the Church. But he did not feel this was a burden, as he often assured those around him, but more a God-given mission, which he therefore carried out joyfully. For this reason John could face nearly all difficulties with ease.

He could never understand how people who held pastoral jobs in the Church could complain about the burden of their pastoral and official tasks. Once a person is called by the Holy Spirit to be a minister, he used to say, he or she must assume the responsibility to preach and to practice the love of one's neighbor. This is not a burden, but a joy.

With this attitude, Pope John did not take himself or the ceremonies and customs of the Vatican too seriously. He often urged those in the papal staff to be less formal with him. When he first got to the Vatican, following his much more serious and more formal predecessor, Pius XII, John's staff was in the habit of kneeling in his presence.

I find it humiliating, he said,
    to see my staff kneel before me.
    My attendants used to kneel three times
        as they arrived in my room
        and again as they left.
I have now gotten them to agree, however,
    that they will genuflect
        once in the morning and again in the evening.
That will be more than enough!

He freely gave permission for people to approach him. And he generally brought a vitality and sense of humor to this entire ancient household. Pope Pius XII had always dined alone, for example, but John loved to share meals. At first, he invited his personal secretary, Monsignor Loris Capovilla, to join him. It didn't take long, however, for this dining circle to widen. Other members of his staff, visitors to the Vatican, and old friends soon sat at the papal table.

He wandered freely through the Vatican gardens, chatting amiably with the staff, getting to know them and asking about their families. Under Pope Pius, this staff was under orders to disappear whenever the pope appeared in the gardens, but John took great joy in being with them.

Stories about this friendly pope quickly leaked out to the world press, and John's popularity grew quickly. He was becoming a worldwide phenomenon, and this added to the expectations for the council he had called. But it was his ability to laugh at himself that made it all possible. He just did not take himself too seriously and certainly did not see himself in the running for sainthood. His journals tell the story of a man who was aware of his own sinfulness and who prayed constantly for grace. He knew himself to be "nothing" and that God provided the power, wisdom, and strength he needed.

John was convinced that the strict guardians of protocol and the suspicious traditionalists among the theologians did not approve of his way of expressing himself or of his behaviors, which did not conform to diplomatic conventions. He was of quick and surprising wit, often seeming to act on the spur of the moment.

The confusion and excitement that surrounds a newly elected pope is enormous. He immediately becomes the public person all the world sees. Within an hour of his election, the waiting crowds in St. Peter's Square meet him— and, with them, all the world—for the first time.

After his election, Pope John was taken into a sacristy to be fitted with the white cassock that he would wear in public the rest of his life. Unfortunately, the Vatican tailor hadn't anticipated someone of Pope John's girth (he weighed over 200 pounds when elected), so the cassock did not fit and was held together with safety pins hidden under a surplice. Shortly after giving his blessing to those around him and receiving the homage of the cardinals of the Church, Pope John came to the central loggia of St. Peter's to meet the crowds, who met him with great enthusiasm and a noisy throng of flashing lights and cameras. Afterward, he tried to describe how he felt at that moment, giving us an insight into the simplicity of heart that he sought for his spiritual journey. Here's a summary of what he said.

All I could think about as I went to this event
were those words of Jesus:
"Learn from me for I am meek and humble of heart."
But as I entered the room
the lights were flashing and people were shouting
and it all resembled the entrance of a movie star!
All I could see were the crowds swaying back and forth.
I gave them my blessing,
but I felt like a blind man.
I could see nothing because of all the television lights.

As I left the event I thought about my new life,
and I realized that from now on,
day in and day out,
people would be looking at me.
I said half aloud to myself,
if you aren't careful to follow Jesus

> with the same humility he had,
> you'll understand nothing
>   and then you'll really be blind!

This ability to see himself as an ordinary person, a fellow traveler on the journey of faith, and a normal guy who puts on his pants every day like everyone else, was a secret key to Pope John's holiness. On January 20, 1959, for example, Pope John got an idea into his head that demonstrates his sense of ordinariness. The pope really cannot leave the Vatican without quite a lot of falderal involving his guards, schedulers, and handlers. Pope John often had his driver take him by car to the Vatican gardens, so it came as no surprise to anyone that one day, the two of them seemed to set out in that direction. Instead, the driver swung the car around the piazza in front of St. Peter's and simply disappeared into the Roman traffic. They had not told anyone where they were headed, nor had they bothered to get an escort from the papal guards. Nobody knew where the pope had gone. Word spread quickly, making Church and government officials all quite frantic. What would the world say if something happened to the pope?

Pope John knew that nothing would happen to him. He just wanted to see some old friends. Word had gotten to Pope John that an old friend, Father Joseph Bergeron of Canada, had wanted to see him but had not asked for an audience because "a humble priest like me should not take up the Holy Father's time." Father Bergeron managed a home for retired Holy Cross priests. The pope's car slowly made its way through the traffic-clogged Roman streets to the old priests' home on Monte Mario. Vatican officials spent their afternoon dealing with hundreds of telephone calls without knowing how to answer the question: "Where is the pope?" Meanwhile, Pope John, having refused the big throne-like chair they offered him, sat in a rocker in a circle of twenty-two very happy old gentlemen, having a lovely time chatting away the afternoon. "Without a little holy folly," he once remarked, "the Church will not enlarge her tabernacles."

Spiritual Exercise

Laugh at yourself

For some of us, laughing at ourselves is very hard to do. For others of us, we wish there weren't so many reasons for it! In any case, part of our spiritual journey is to develop a sense of humor. Laughing at ourselves is not the same as poking fun at others. Making jokes about others can sometimes be mean and an expression of power over them. But sharing funny moments when we were foolish, mistaken, accidentally out of sync, or just silly is different.

Like it did for Pope John, self-deprecating humor will disarm anyone who wants to overpower us with mean words or unkindness. It allows us to relax and trust the flow of life, even when we aren't perfect or correct. This exercise will help us hone the art of kindly laughing at oneself.

Step One » *Begin in prayer.*
Ask God to open your heart to his word, which is being spoken to you in the depths of your own heart. Pray that you might hear the divine voice. Pray also for discernment to help you distinguish God's voice from the din of other voices that may be calling you to selfish thoughts and actions.

Step Two » *Give yourself permission to laugh at yourself.*

Pope John looked into a mirror shortly after they dressed him in his white papal garments and said, half to himself, that he knew he would never look good in front of all those TV cameras. He had given himself permission to see himself as imperfect but still fully lovable and capable.

Uncover your sense of humor by reducing your drive for perfection. I know the text of Matthew 5:48 demands that we all "be perfect" but the deeper meaning of the Greek work used in the original text is that we make being Godlike our goal. We can do that (seriously!) while still having a light-hearted approach whenever possible. Here's how *The Message* translates that phrase:

> *In a word, what I'm saying is,* Grow up. *You're kingdom subjects. Now live like it. Live out your God-created identity. Live generously and graciously toward others, the way God lives toward you.*

Here's your exercise: Tell yourself that it really is OK for you to laugh at yourself. You may need to convince yourself of this. For example, recently I was shopping for some used items in a second-hand store. As I went to check out, the young clerk (much younger than I!) said, "If you're a senior citizen, you get a 10% discount here." Then she paused and eyed me. "I'll just go ahead and give it to you," she said. Apparently I looked old enough. I went home and peered into my mirror. When did I get to be so old? Good grief.

Take just a moment to affirm that you need not be perfect— that you can indeed laugh at your foibles and imperfections.

Step Three » *Look back, but just briefly.*
Pause in your day to look back over things and find the humor

that's there. Even in terribly difficult times, if we turn worry into humor and see the odd predicaments in which we sometimes find ourselves, there is a reason to laugh. Go ahead and do it; give your laughter muscles a daily workout.

After he was elected, Pope John had many sleepless nights. An immense burden had been given to him and he was already seventy-eight years old. One night he was half-awake, thinking about something, and he muttered to himself, "I'll have to talk that over with the pope." Then he roused himself a bit more and said half-aloud again, "Oh my! I'm the pope. I guess I'll have to talk it over with the Lord."

Here's your exercise: Think back over the past two or three days. Identify several encounters, incidents, or events that you were part of. Note them. Look at them carefully now, and tell yourself or someone else what humor you saw in them. For example, recently I visited a dear, lifelong friend who had landed in a hospital with a serious but curable kidney ailment. After our greeting, he turned to me and said, "Aren't we a fine pair: me with half a kidney and you with half a mind?"

Take another moment to bring to mind the odd moments of your past days.

Step Four » *God help you.*
At times of stress, even great and challenging times, notice the funny aspects of them, and allow laughter to reduce the anxiety of the moment. One day, Pope John came to the door of the Holy Spirit Hospital in Rome to visit an old friend who was there. The sisters who managed the hospital weren't expecting him, but the one in charge—full of stress and not sure what to say—went up to introduce herself. She said something like, "Welcome, Holy Father, I am the superior of the Holy Spirit." Pope John replied in his usual self-deprecating humor, saying something like, "Well,

that's wonderful for you, Sister, I'm only the vicar of Christ."

Here's your exercise: No matter what the setting, keep an eye out for ways in which appropriate humor can lead to healing. Convert potential hurt or anger into humor. For example, I was recently leading a team workshop for a parish staff on which there was clear division about pastoral approaches. As I started the workshop, I really had to convince myself we would find humor that day. Sure enough, we did and the humor created an environment in which everyone felt safe to explore the differences and choose an agreed path forward.

Thinking back now, revisit the people, events, or situations that came to mind for you earlier. Think about how you might have turned tension or mistakes into laughter and lightness. Ask Jesus Christ to come to you and give you the grace of pure happiness, expressed in a jovial and pleasant ability to take lightly these things in your life.

Chapter 7

HOLY POVERTY

Pope John was born to a working-class family that did not even own the land they farmed. He was one of a dozen children, although only nine survived childhood. If you could go back to 1881, the year of his birth, and step into the farm house into which he was born, you would consider their living conditions to be grinding poverty. The cattle and other farm animals lived on the ground floor of this house, which was common. It would be a long time before electricity would reach the rural hamlet of Sotto il Monte near Bergamo in northern Italy. Pope John's parents were Marianna and Giovanni, also called Battista. His dad farmed, working the land mainly by hand each day. His mom raised the children. They shared this house with Luigi and Carissimi, Giovanni's brother and his wife, who also had ten children, so it was a crowded house. There were about thirty at the supper table every evening.

Pope John often referred with pride to the poverty of his family home. In that home, he learned to trust God's providence. They were sharecroppers, giving up to half their annual yield to the lord on whose land they lived. Only later did political reform give them the ability to own the land. Life moved slowly here. People rarely left the village or traveled far. It had been like this since the 800s. Time nearly stood still in Sotto il Monte. They were poor and humble peasants, but they were not destitute. They had well-tilled land and vineyards; cattle for cream, butter, and veal; and many hands to make lighter work. This was a life saturated with meaning. God's hand was seen in every day's work, and each evening ended with the entire family praying the rosary, kneeling in the crowded farmhouse. God spoke through this natural environment. Every season of the year, each feast of the Church, and everyone who came and went represented the movement of God. Their simple life, lived in a way that sustained their land, was the first avenue toward sainthood that Angelo walked as a nineteenth-century farm boy.

Pope John knew that if we wish to understand God's word, the first requirement is poverty. By this we don't mean to suggest that destitution is the value we cherish, but that living simply, sustainably, and in solidarity with the poor certainly is. We are bound by the gospel and our own social teaching to eradicate destitution. But living simply without seeking great wealth is a form of poverty that makes the soul noble and the spiritual life rich. Here is a summary of Pope John's comments about this.

I am very happy to be able to say to Christ,
    "I am here in the state in which
        you chose to place me."
I am satisfied, and I plan to remain faithful to you
        no matter what.
From this simple life I learn humility,
        I learn about purity of heart,
        about hard work and self-sacrifice.
If I have anything of value in this world

let me share it with others.
That some people grow rich while others live in misery
   violates divine law.
And we know that the greedy ones
   are not easy in their mind
   but have a lingering guilt that makes them unhappy.
But when we practice generosity and kindness,
   when we show a cheerful spirit,
   then we find harmony and peace!

The older I get the more I realize
   that the best way to remain holy
   is to reduce everything—
      plans, ambitions, and money—
      to the simplest level.
Like a vine that needs trimming,
   so must I trim my own life
   to make sure I'm not selfish but generous.
Any other way of life leads to unhappiness.
My own sense of simplicity and humility
   has always been my good companion.

Because I was raised in poverty and humility
   in Sotto il Monte,
   I have always tried to draw lessons from it.
From that childhood came many wonderful gifts:
   parish priests who became models for me,
   wonderful parents who loved me unconditionally,
   deep roots in the teachings of Jesus Christ,
   and the ability to be content with what I have.
Born poor I can also now prepare to die poor.
   Everything I have gathered

(and there wasn't much)
has now been given to others.

In these remarks, Pope John is teaching us that our own small-ness is actually a gift. Simple living allows us to focus on others and their needs. It allows us the time to read, pray, and grow in our faith. It provides a life that is not ostentatious. Ostentatious lives need a lot of maintenance. There is no end of the show they are required to put on. Living simply, sustainably, and in solidarity with the poor leads, on the other hand, to the greatest human happiness that can be attained.

Spiritual Exercise

LIVE SIMPLY

Step One » *Begin in prayer.*
Ask God to open your heart to his word, which is being spoken to you in the depths of your own heart. Pray that you might hear the divine voice. Pray also for discernment to help you distinguish God's voice from the din of other voices that may be calling you to selfish thoughts and actions.

Step Two » *Read the story of the rich young man from Matthew 19:16–26.*

> *Another day, a man stopped Jesus and asked, "Teacher, what good thing must I do to get eternal life?" Jesus said, "Why do you question me about what's good? God is the One who is good. If you want to enter the life of God, just do what he tells you." The*

man asked, "What in particular?"

Jesus said, "Don't murder, don't commit adultery, don't steal, don't lie, honor your father and mother, and love your neighbor as you do yourself." The young man said, "I've done all that. What's left?"

"If you want to give it all you've got," Jesus replied, "go sell your possessions; give everything to the poor. All your wealth will then be in heaven. Then come follow me."

That was the last thing the young man expected to hear. And so, crestfallen, he walked away. He was holding on tight to a lot of things, and he couldn't bear to let go.

As he watched him go, Jesus told his disciples, "Do you have any idea how difficult it is for the rich to enter God's kingdom? Let me tell you, it's easier to gallop a camel through a needle's eye than for the rich to enter God's kingdom."

The disciples were staggered. "Then who has any chance at all?" Jesus looked hard at them and said, "No chance at all if you think you can pull it off yourself. Every chance in the world if you trust God to do it."

Step Three 〉 *Your exercise.*
In your imagination, see yourself in the place of this rich young man. When one thinks about it, most of us actually are very well-fed, clothed, and cared for. Compared to most of the people

of the world, we live in great comfort. So make yourself a rich young man or woman and go to Jesus, seeking greater happiness and fulfillment. Ask him what is needed for you to achieve it.

Pause here to put yourself in the place of this story. Say the words to Jesus aloud. If you are in a place that lacks privacy, say them aloud to yourself or write them.

Step Four » *Listen.*

What do you believe God is calling you to in regard to your own money, no matter how much or how little you have?

Chapter 8

HOLY UNITY
IN CHRIST

After the first session of Vatican II closed, the bishops of the world left Rome and returned to their respective dioceses. They had all been gone for more than two months, and there was a backlog for them of ordinations, confirmations, appointments, and public liturgies. During this period, Pope John wrote a personal and intimate letter to them, which was sent in January 1963, just five months before his death. The letter discussed a new commission of cardinals who would direct the work of the second session, suggested how the world's bishops living far from Rome during the recess would keep in touch with the development of Council matters, affirmed the emerging cooperation between clergy and laity in the Council, and reflected on some of the achievements and hopes of the Council.

In the latter section, Pope John wrote about the historic participation of all the Christians of the world in Vatican II. Indeed, this was the first such instance of cooperation in more than a thousand years! A thousand years! Centuries of grudges were coming to a swift end. Here is what he wrote, in part, in summary form:

At first, the plan to hold an ecumenical council
    did not attract much attention
    from the people of the world.
But after all the preparation we did together,
    and now since the first session,
    which ended in December 1962,
        we see almost universal interest
        in what we're doing,
        even from those of other religions.
We might say that the light of heavenly grace
    has cast its rays closer than ever
    to the minds of all people,
        drawing them ever closer to Christ and the Church.
For example, we invited our separated sisters and brothers
    to come to Rome
    and take part in the Council
        and they all attended!
This is really a unique moment in history
    and we take this to be a sign
    that all people of faith, including us,
    are ready to end division and join in unity.
After all, didn't Jesus pray for this
    in John 17?
        "Father, it's time.
        Display the bright splendor of your Son
        So the Son in turn may show your bright splendor.
        I pray for...those you gave me,
        For they are yours by right.
        Holy Father, guard them as they pursue this life
        That you conferred as a gift through me,

So they can be one heart and mind
As we are one heart and mind" (John 17:1, 9, 11).
That many of our separated sisters and brothers
see the Council in such a positive light
gives me great hope.
This hope will grow even more if we can join together
and form one Christian family,
"one fold and one shepherd" (John 10:16).

The key shift that Pope John brought to the discussion of Christian unity was his use of a new language, a language that focused on love rather than on legal reunification. This marked a significant change in attitude and, in the end, pervaded Vatican II's discussion of unity. In part, this emerged from Pope John's own generous attitude toward the world and those around him. In part, it emerged from his own faith, for he firmly believed Christian unity was not an optional dimension of his program, not an agenda item for the Council, but the chief work of his pontificate. He firmly believed that there would be one flock and one shepherd, not out of human desire but because Jesus Christ wishes it to be so. Who are we, he asked, to argue with that?

Knowing the propensity of his colleagues in the Vatican to argue the fine points of any theological position based on scholastic scholarship or the teachings of popes over the centuries, Pope John studiously avoided any description of unity that might have contained in itself a theological position. He used a rich blend of analogies with language drawn largely from the gospels—less to initiate politico-ecclesiastic activity as to encourage love.

Pope John believed that the world community could not be at peace and join together in peaceful initiatives rather than war until the Christians of the world came together in harmony.

The unity of Christians thus became a fervent hope of his and is closely linked to his desire for world peace.

Spiritual Exercise

Unity among the people with whom you live

Step One » *Begin in prayer.*
Ask God to open your heart to his word, which is being spoken to you in the depths of your own heart. Pray that you might hear the divine voice. Pray also for discernment to help you distinguish God's voice from the din of other voices that may be calling you to selfish thoughts and actions.

Step Two » *Read article 4 of the Decree on Ecumenism from Vatican II.*
This section of the decree spells out for us the work that must be done in order to move toward greater unity. Such unity among Christians may be established, in part, by official dialogue at the high levels of theology, praxis, and church governance. But such unity is also established as Christians of good will from all faith traditions come together to love each other with charity and tenderness, to work together for justice and peace which knows no sectarian boundaries, and to pray together to the one Christ whom we all adore.

Here is a summary of article 4:

The work of ecumenism is really the work of the Holy Spirit. All over the world, people are engaged in prayer, words, and actions in order to obtain full Christian unity, and it is the Holy Spirit that draws us together. We bishops of the Second Vatican Council wish to affirm such efforts on the part of Catholics and encourage them to continue their work. We all dream of a unity among Christians that will strengthen the unity of the whole world.

In today's ecumenical movement, specific efforts are being made to make this dream of unity a reality for the whole Church. The efforts that individuals and groups are taking include five important elements:

First, people are nurturing a sense of truth about various denominations rather than proceeding with past prejudices and false perceptions.

Second, they are joining together in dialogue in order to gain a greater appreciation of the richness of each denomination.

Third, they are cooperating with one another to address the pressing needs of society around them, thus building the Kingdom of God.

Fourth, they are joining hearts together in prayer.

And fifth, they are humbly examining their own religion to determine if it is in line with the will of Christ. If it is not, they are then making efforts for reform where necessary.

These and other actions, when carried out under the guidance of the Holy Spirit and the leadership of the Church, promote justice and truth. Little by little, this will lead to full Christian unity. One day, all Christians will gather together to celebrate the Eucharist as God's one and holy Church. Such unity can already be found in the Catholic Church, and we must make every effort to make this unity increase until it is full and complete.

While it is important for Catholics to be concerned about their sisters and brothers in other churches and to invite them to know the Catholic Church, our primary responsibility as Catholics is to make sure that our own household is in order. Only when we confront our own shortcomings and make the necessary reforms will we truly be able to discern the will of Christ and bear witness to Christ's teaching. Yes, through the grace of God, the Catholic Church has maintained the truth that was first given to us. But through shortcomings, stubbornness, and sin, the Catholic Church as a whole and the individual members within it have often failed to understand this truth and to live by it. Sometimes we have moved away from God's reign rather than moved toward it.

The role of each member, then, is to aim at Christian perfection. All in the Church must try to live freely, listening for the voice of the Holy Spirit. They must give expression to the authentic prompting of this Spirit, which will lead all to see the true nature of the Catholic Church. The Catholic Church is unified yet diverse, embracing all cultures yet true to our apostolic roots.

Catholics seek Christ wherever he can be found and gratefully acknowledge the ways that other denominations contribute to our understanding of the Christian mission. Catholics realize that any action grounded in authentic faith is for the good of God's one Church.

The separation that the Church is presently experiencing is more than just an unfortunate situation. It prevents the Church from fully realizing its true nature as truly *catholic,* a word which means "universal." It prevents us from truly being one household of faith living in the family of God. Therefore, this council once again wishes to commend those who are involved in the vital work of ecumenism and to encourage all to take an active role in reconciling our differences.

Step Three » *Pause and look back over this text.*
What phrases or words stick in your mind? What key message do they have for you?

Step Four » *Prayer.*
Ask Christ to lead you to actions on behalf of ecumenism. What neighbor, family member, friend, or colleague can you welcome more fully in God's name? How can you express the love of Christ for all in a more profound way toward those who are separated from the Catholic Church, either because they are in other Christian churches or because they are simply no longer active in the Catholic faith?

Pause to call them to mind now along with your commitment to love them.

Close with this prayer from Pope John:

O eternal Word of God,
    Son of God and Son of Mary,
Renew again deep within us the miracles of your birth,
    your self-giving love,
      and your self-emptying death and resurrection.
Fill us with charity toward one another
    and gather us all in the unity
    of your body, the Body of Christ.
Thus may your presence among us
    establish forever the peace and love
    of your holy family. Amen.

HOLY JUSTICE (WITHIN OUR OWN HOUSE)

P ope John was well aware that, for many centuries, very little had been modernized in the inner workings of the Vatican itself. Changes of any kind had come only very, very slowly to the ancient papal household. Sometimes this resulted in a serious deterioration of justice to those lay people who worked in the Vatican.

Meanwhile, he himself had spent much of his career working in various roles within the Church, roles that brought him very close to the workings of the society around him. He hadn't been at the Vatican very long when he began to realize that the Church itself did not always live up to the standards to which it called others.

One day, while an electrician was installing telephones, Pope John went to chat with him. "How are things going?" asked the pope.

"Badly, badly, your Eminence," said the electrician, thinking he was speaking with a cardinal. Seeing that he looked tired and thin, the pope asked about his family and his work. The man poured out his tale of struggle against grinding poverty while surviving on Vatican City wages.

"We'll have to do something about this," he was assured. "For just between you and me, I'm not 'Your Eminence.' I'm the pope."

John XXIII had discovered a disconnection between Church teaching and practice. Since Pope Leo XIII in the late nineteenth century, the Church had been teaching about the rights of workers and the duties of employers. But apparently the Church itself had not lived up to its own teachings. And, indeed, within a short time, wages for Vatican workers were raised. Employees who were being paid the least received the largest advances in salary, and extra allowances were given them as well when called for by the number of children at home. When some in the higher ranks complained, Pope John told them, "One man's learning calls for reward, but another man's need can be even more urgent." And when he was told that Vatican finances could not support these increases and that the Vatican's direct charitable gifts would have to be cut back to afford them, Pope John said, "Then we'll have to cut them. For this raise is simple justice, and justice comes before charity."

By this simple act, Pope John demonstrated his commitment to justice far more dramatically than a thousand pages of well-crafted papal pronouncements could have done. Those around him came to understand his priorities, his disdain for centuries-old customs that no longer met current demands, and his belief that human needs precede protocol.

In his own words, summarized here, Pope John teaches us about justice.

How can we ask others
> to follow the teaching of the Church
> regarding social justice
if we ourselves do not apply them in our own house?
> Indeed, we must be the first,
> we must take the lead by our own example.
We must write our checks as we do our pastoral letters!

Justice, we know,
> comes to us from God's own wisdom
> and it means we must
> give everyone his or her due compensation.
We begin by admitting that everything we have
> comes to us from the Creator;
> God is the source of everything.
Secondly, we realize with full force
> that we are bound to follow the teachings
> of the Master, Jesus Christ.
These teachings are now two thousand years old
> and they remain as true as ever;
> they lead us to justice and love.
Sometimes we have not lived them very well,
> and sometimes we have failed even
> to teach them fully.
But nonetheless, we are required
> to treat others with love
> and put their needs before our own.
We are required to leave no one out
> when the goods of the earth are shared.
Our own hope for eternal life
> rests squarely on how we treat each other,

on how we treat "the least of Christ's kin."
Therefore, let us practice justice
  as a central part of our faith,
  on a par with all doctrine and dogma.

Spiritual Exercise

Examine what you own

Step One » *Begin in prayer.*
Ask God to open your heart to his word, which is being spoken
to you in the depths of your own heart. Pray that you might
hear the divine voice. Pray also for discernment to help you
distinguish God's voice from the din of other voices that may
be calling you to selfish thoughts and actions.

Step Two » *Put pencil to paper.*
This is an active exercise that will require you to have a pad of
paper and a good, sharp pencil. On the paper, draw a line to
create two columns. Now walk through your home and note
what you have there. List everything (yes, every pair of shoes!)
in the left-hand column. This may take you quite a while if you
are wealthy and own many things. Let the time this takes you
form the first part of your exercise. Don't skip anything. Visit
the storage areas—those especially—since this is where you may
have many items you no longer use. Look through your kitchen
at all the food you own.

Also consult your bank and retirement fund statements. Note
how much money you have there.

Of course, for some people, this exercise will not take very
long. They have no permanent home and must seek a place to

sleep each evening. All they own may fit into a single shopping cart or garbage bag. For others, unless they have just returned home from the local food shelf, their kitchens have very little in them. And for still others, they have been under- or unemployed and have had to sell some of their most prized possessions in order to pay the mortgage or rent.

Pause now to make your list. Be careful not to skip anything. If you live with others, invite them to participate with you in doing this.

Step Three » *Meet the poor.*
Once you have your list, pause, as Pope John did, to meet the ones who have less than you. Get to know them by name. Learn about their families and the difficulty they may have in providing for them.

Prayerfully read through your list again and again. Ask the Holy Spirit to guide you as you decide what you are entitled to keep and what you are called to give to others. Circle the items you will give away.

Step Four » *Close now by reflecting on this teaching of Pope John:*
One day, while walking in the papal gardens with his secretary, Monsignor Loris Capovilla, Pope John was listening to some of his recent notes being read in preparation for upcoming work. In the course of this reading, and while admiring the beauty of Michelangelo's dome lit by the sun, Pope John stopped still. A particular sentence caught his ear from St. John Chrysostom, which we read, in summary:

Christ has left us on this earth
    and asked us to become shining beacons and teachers;

he asked us to be his messengers to all people;
he wants us to win them over to his teachings.
It would not even be necessary for us to teach our doctrine,
    if we all lived in this way.
We would need no words to preach the gospel
    if our deeds showed the way.
"There would be no pagans if we all behaved
        like real Christians."

There were a few moments of silence. Then Pope John said,
This is the truth:
    Anyone who asks
    what I tried to accomplish as pope,
    may be given this as the answer.
    "That is all there is to it."

Chapter 10

HOLY PEACE

To say that the promotion of peace—peace within men and women, social peace, and international peace—was important to Pope John is to understate its priority in his papacy. He turned to this theme repeatedly in both public and private decisions and remarks.

For example, on October 12, 1962, the day after the opening of Vatican II, he addressed diplomats from seventy-nine nations who had sent one kind of delegate or another to the Vatican for the events. Vatican II would be a religious event, he told them, but he also hoped it would contribute to the development of world peace. This peace, he said, should be "based on growing respect for the human person and leading to freedom of religion and worship." Sitting there in the room was the diplomat from the United States, G. Frederick Reinhardt, who perhaps knew that, within the week, the Cuban missile crisis would overtake the world, bringing it to the edge of war.

It was in the midst of that crisis, on October 25, that Pope John conceived the idea to write an encyclical on war and peace—*Pacem in Terris*, as it would later be named. Within three weeks,

Pope John learned from his doctors that his cancer was serious and that he had less than a year to live. Remarkably, John became more determined than ever to write the encyclical. He may not live to see the end of his Council, he must have decided, but he could at least complete work on this important document.

Despite his serious illness, which often filled him with pain, Pope John's passion to complete this message to the world did not wane. He saw this as a way to extend the love of Christ to the world, and he was committed to doing so.

Up to this time, encyclicals had normally been sent to the world's bishops, but this one was addressed to everyone in the world, whether Catholic or not. What surprises the reader, though, is that the letter is written in John's own personal style, in his words. It avoids the formal and high prose that papal writers usually use. In it, he did something no pope had done before him. He spelled out a series of human rights that, he said, are the basis of a lasting peace. The first right he named is the right to worship as one chooses, an issue over which the bishops of the Council spent a good deal of time arguing. He added the right to engage in politics as one pleases, to have safety and security for immigrants and refugees, and the right of even small nations to self-determination.

Of course, such rights bring with them clear obligations. Large and wealthy nations are obliged to care for smaller and poorer ones, he says. All governments must be concerned first and foremost with the economic progress and technical skills of their people. He listed four pillars of a peaceful society: truth, justice, love, and freedom.

The following spring, on May 13, 1962, Cardinal Suenens of Belgium represented Pope John in New York City at the United Nations, where he delivered and presented to this world body the official copy of this rare papal document, addressed as it was to all the people of the earth and not merely to Catholics. *Pacem in Terris*, Suenens told the UN, may be called a "symphony for peace," like Beethoven's Ninth. Its theme is peace, he told them, which needs truth as its foundation, justice as its norm, love as its driving force, and freedom as its setting.

Human efforts in the matter of universal peacemaking are still far from the point where heaven and earth meet. The fact is that true peace cannot come, save from God. It has only one name: the peace of Christ. It has one aspect, that impressed on it by Christ who, as if to anticipate the counterfeits of humans, emphasized, "Peace I leave with you, my peace I give to you" (John 14:27).

On Christmas Day 1959, Pope John spoke to the entire world via radio, and his message was all about this peace. Here, in part and in summary form, is what he said.

Peace is a gift from God like no other
    and it's also the condition of life
    for which modern women and men long.
All aspects of true peace must flow together
    in order for peace to be lasting.

The first aspect is peace of heart.
    Before all else, peace is an interior state,
    rooted in a sense of well-being
        that flows from divine love.
When one follows his or her conscience
    there is interior peace
    that cannot be destroyed.
Because in our conscience we hear the voice of God
    echoing in the depths of our souls,
    we are always led by it to love and peace.

But when we disobey our conscience
    there is interior disorder leading to hate,
        self-hate, and violence toward others.

The second aspect is social peace
    which flows from having respect
    for the dignity of all men and women.
We assert strongly that each and every human being
    deserves to live with dignity
    and should not be treated as less-than-human.
When persons are treated well
    there is no need for violence or uprising.
Everything in every nation should be addressed
    toward the care of the people,
        above institutions, businesses, or the state.
When humans are treated as machines
    and become a mere bit of merchandise,
    social peace cannot be achieved,
        and violence results.
This means we must encourage a sense of community
    and the common good
    among all the people of the nation.
Knowing they belong to each other
    will help end greed and the desire to dominate.

The third aspect is international peace.
    When men and women are at personal peace
    and the nation establishes dignity for all,
    then this same nation must live in peace with others.
We must give up the false idea
    that force is justified or
    that nationalism trumps peace.

It is justice between nations
   that makes peace a solid reality.
People who are treated justly
   do not move toward war.
And justice, in turn, is based on charity.
   When men and women love others
   they care for them generously
   and do not live selfishly.
We speak, then, of actually *living together*
   and not merely of *coexisting*.

We believe that these three—
   personal peace,
   social peace,
   and international peace—
      are interlocked with each other.
We summon all on earth
   to help establish this threefold peace
   because when we do,
      then we will achieve
      what God desires for the human race.

Spiritual Exercise

MOVEMENT TOWARD PEACE

Step One » *As always, begin in prayer.*
Ask God to open your heart to his word, which is being spoken
to you in the depths of your own heart. Pray that you might
hear the divine voice. Pray also for discernment to help you
distinguish God's voice from the din of other voices that may

be calling you to selfish thoughts and actions.

Step Two » *Inner peace.*

Interior peace results from knowing and accepting the pathway that God sets out for you. In other words, when you follow your conscience, paying attention to your true sense of right or wrong, good or evil, you are at peace, no matter what else may happen. This was the secret of Pope John's success as a leader. He allowed humility and obedience to lead him. His motto, in fact, was "Obedience and Peace." If we trust that the universe is unfolding as it should and that we are playing the part in it to which we are called, then we can relax our worry and allow ourselves to be at peace.

Your exercise: List those things about which you are worried. Is someone near you sick? Are you short of funds? Do you feel unattractive to others? Is your car breaking down? Did you make someone angry? Are you lonely? Simply list for yourself those things that cause you to worry.

Pause now to make this list. You may want to go for a walk, spend time in the chapel, or even chat with a close friend in order to make the list complete.

Step Three » *Evaluate each item.*

- Circle the item if it is something you cannot change (such as other people, the weather, the course of international events, the past right up to this very minute, or others).

- If the item is something to which you realize that worry adds nothing, cross it out by putting a line through it. Often, achieving inner peace means we have to trust that the universe is indeed unfolding as intended. Your worry doesn't help it much.

- If the item is something you could make a plan to resolve, draw a rectangle around it. If you have angered someone, plan to reconcile. If you are short of funds, plan to tighten your belt or add to your income. And so forth.

Step Four » *Social peace.*
Your exercise: Think about those people with whom you are not at peace. Maybe forgiveness is needed. Maybe you've been hurt by them. Maybe they've encroached on your space or time. Maybe you consider them morally inferior to you. Just list them all and give the reason you feel at odds with them.

Pause now to create this list. We sometimes block unhappy memories or events from our minds, so you need to be very honest and search deeply to make sure this list is complete.

Step Five » *Reflection.*
Now return to this list as you did the one above and note one way you could be the big one, die to yourself, make them first and you last, or forgive them seventy times seven times. In other words, note ways in which you can practice the art of self-giving love with them. Think about Jesus Christ and his cross in this exercise and imitate him. Imitate the way in which he emptied himself. He gave up his very life, but he never, ever gave up his love.

Social peace results from imitating Christ in his paschal mystery. You may want to begin to take steps to forgive, reconcile, or reunite with some people. With others you may simply offer them to the Lord but continue to keep your distance. Or you may want to take this worksheet with you to celebrate the sacrament of reconciliation.

Chapter 11

HOLINESS LEADS TO AN OPEN LIFE

Near the end of his life it was decided that a bust of Pope John should be cast as a lasting memorial of him. This is a common-enough practice among key public figures, but Pope John turned this occasion, like all others he touched, into an opportunity for charity.

The sculptor chosen for the work was from John's own home area of Bergamo in northern Italy. His name: Giacomo Manzu. This sculptor was not, initially, a man of faith, and he would not have been the first choice of most members of the pope's staff. Pope John had been told beforehand about this man's opinions of the Church and its clergy—opinions that tended toward the negative. Beyond that, Manzu lived a life quite out-side "Catholic norms" in terms of his relationships, his politics, and his churchgoing.

But, nonetheless, Manzu was chosen. He and Pope John worked together to produce the bust. Pope John posed. Manzu sketched and molded clay. Meanwhile, the conversation in the room was producing a lasting friendship.

After the first day of posing, Pope John sensed what the sculptor had been feeling: the need for them to know one another better. Pope John may have also felt lonely; he often said that he felt the papacy was very isolating for a man of his friendly inclinations. He seemed to see in Manzu someone who would not be too impressed with his position as pope, someone with whom he could relate on a more personal, ordinary level.

So, despite the carefully guarded privacy around the pope's apartment in the Vatican, he took Manzu there and gave him a remarkably complete tour of the place. During the tour—which included the contents of the closets!—Pope John offered Manzu his own very self, the "stuff" of his life, rather than of his important position of pope. Manzu accepted, looking into the ordinary daily life of Pope John as a friend would do.

The tour covered photos of Pope John's family, stories of his friends, mementos of previous assignments—the kind of "stuff" you'd expect to find in anyone's apartment. Both men showed the essential first element necessary for moving from "official relationships" to real ones: interest in each other. They paid attention to each other. And, in the end, both were richer.

They slowly made their way around the room, looking at this and that. At last, they reach the clothes closet. Pope John paused at the door and then opened it, almost as though he was also curious to see inside. There were a lot of church and papal garments: the white papal robes he wore, a red shoulder cape, a cloak for cold weather, and then, on a bottom shelf, two rows of papal slippers. They were red and white and on each one was sewn a golden cross. There was a pair of green ones, too, and all together it made a brilliant array. But it also seemed to leave the pope uneasy.

"These are the shoes they've given me," he said, and looked at his visitor.

Manzu looked at the shoes and nodded. Sometimes words just aren't needed. They were both examining the same thing.

"They don't really fit me very well," the pope said.

Manzu nodded again, knowingly. "They look narrow and tight," he said.

"They are awful," Pope John told him. "The best shoes I ever had were in the Italian army. We Roncallis all have big feet and those were just right. You could walk in them for miles and miles and hardly feel it."

There was a silence, and Manzu added: "These must be hard to walk in."

"Terrible," John said. "But I think it's part of the conspiracy here to prevent me from walking out of the Vatican. Every time I leave the papal grounds, they get excited as though Italy was too dangerous for a Pope."

There was also a tiara in the closet, a very ornate one covered in stones and encircled with gold and silver bands. It was very heavy, but Pope John took it down and handed it to Manzu. "This was a gift from the good people of Bergamo," he told him, "but it's too heavy to wear. Here, lift it yourself," he said, handing it over.

Manzu took it from John and it really was quite heavy. "*Porca miseria!*" he exclaimed in his native Italian. He had forgotten that he was with the pope. His curse involved the name of God, and he was asking God to damn something. But Pope John closed his eyes gently and responded to the literal words, saying "Well, there's no misery here, except maybe my own poor self, unable to bear up under what they expect of me!"

"Thank you, Holiness," Manzu said, handing back the tiara.

Finally they came to the pope's bed. It was very plain, made of mahogany. On a bedside table, Manzu noticed a phone and a few books. This seemed to be the most intimate part of the tour. Here the pope, for all his daytime power, slept in his pajamas— no crown, no slippers, no assistants. He simply went to bed like everyone else in Rome, or in the whole world, for that matter.

On the wall opposite the bed stood a *prie-dieu,* and above it was hanging a simple crucifix, which Pope John had not pointed out during the tour. This is where the pope began each day, in silent prayer with God. Why had he not bothered to show this to Manzu? A farmer, giving a tour of his land, would show the crops, his family, and his barns, but he would not stop and point to the sun in the sky. The sun is the center and source of it all. It's too obvious. Pope John looked up at the crucifix now, his face full of simple wonderment, the sort of expression one might have if one looked at a gorgeous sunset.

In that moment like none before it, Manzu had what he needed to finish the sculpture. It was the expression on Pope John's face. His features showed his strength, his tender love, his self-denial, his humble origins—this is what made the man, what made Angelo Roncalli.

Your Exercise

A PRIVATE TOUR

Step One » *As always, begin in prayer.*
Ask God to open your heart to his word, which is being spoken to you in the depths of your own heart. Pray that you might hear the divine voice. Pray also for discernment to help you distinguish God's voice from the din of other voices that may be calling you to selfish thoughts and actions.

Step Two » *A visit.*

Imagine that you were getting your home ready for a visit by one of your great heroes or heroines. Who would it be for you? Who would you most like to come for a visit to your home? Would it be Jesus himself? Pope John? Some other historical figure? Or maybe it would be a living person: a president, artist, actor, or long-lost friend.

Pause and bring to mind that person. In your imagination, invite them to come for a visit.

Now think about the place where you live. What would you need to change there before such a visit? What would you hide, or bring out of storage to display?

Take just a moment to think about your home and bring it to mind.

Now begin the tour, much as Pope John had done. Meet your guest at the door, welcome them, and show them your home, telling the story of what they will find there. Share your personal thoughts about it all, the elements that you like, those that may embarrass you, a little story connected to this or that item. Is there something like the crucifix, something that symbolizes that around which you organize your life? What would that be for you, in all honesty.

Likewise, introduce your guest to the people who live there with you. Who are they? With what words would you introduce them?

Step Three » *Prayer.*

When you are finished and have said your farewell, turn your thoughts to Jesus Christ. Thank him for the gift of everyday life, the life you lead day in and day out. Invite him to lead you through this to greater self-giving love, greater holiness. Tell him whatever is in your heart at this moment.

Take time now to be in dialogue with God.

Chapter 12

MY BAGS ARE PACKED FOR HOLY DEATH

E ven though the official Vatican spokesperson refused to admit it, by the end of May 1963, everyone knew that Pope John lay dying. Reports circu-
lated around the world, and people from far and
wide began to keep vigil in St. Peter's Square. The
crowds there grew day by day into the thousands. The world
kept vigil under his window. He had touched so many people,
Catholic and non-Catholic. They knew that he loved them no
matter who they were or what they believed.

Ten years before his death, dying had been on Pope John's
mind. Here is what he wrote in his journal then (in 1952):

I should always be mindful of my death.
  The end is drawing nearer
  as my days follow one another.
I want to concern myself with dying well

rather than dreaming of a longer life.
This does not make me sad, because
  I am following the will of God.
But in view of my death,
    I have stopped worrying about receiving accolades,
    and I have stopped thinking about those
        with whom I disagree.
I only want one thing at this point,
    which is that my life should end in a holy way.
I do fear that the pain will be more than I can handle
    but I also trust that God walks with me.

In the decade after he wrote these words, of course, a great deal
more was given to him by God. He was called to serve as the pa-
triarch of Venice the very next year. And in 1958, he was called
again to serve: as Pope John XXIII. He opened the Second Vatican
Council against terribly steep odds—his own Vatican corps was
largely opposed to the idea, and many of them did not support the
outcomes enthusiastically. As he lay dying in early 1963, he gave
the world the gift of *Pacem in Terris*, his last testament.

By late May 1963, his pain was tremendous as he struggled
against his cancer, but one morning he was feeling better, and his
longtime companion and secretary, Monsignor Loris Capovilla,
read to him from *The Imitation of Christ* and from the countless
get-well messages that had come in from around the world, from
the famous and the ordinary.

By May 30, John's doctors realized there was nothing more
they could do to prolong his life. Monsignor Capovilla broke the
news to him that the end was at hand. Pope John asked only that
he be aided to die with grace. Slowly he met in farewell audience
with his family and staff, one after the other, as he ebbed into
and out of sometimes painful, and sometimes peaceful, sleep.

At 11:00 AM on May 31, Pope John addressed those keeping closest vigil with him. In part he said:

My secret strength has always come
    from that crucifix you see opposite my bed.
I see it the moment I awake
    and again before going to sleep.
I have spent long hours in dialogue with the Lord.
    See this crucifix as I do:
    the open arms have been the program
        which I pursued as pope.
They tell us that Christ died for all, for all,
    excluding no one.
Everyone is offered his love and forgiveness. Everyone.

My time is now drawing to a close
    but Christ lives on in the Church.
    That all may be one, is my final prayer.
        One in Christ.

On the night of Pentecost, June 2, twenty thousand young people in Milan spent the night in the cathedral there praying for him. Cardinal Montini was among them. We need, Montini told them, "to gather up his inheritance and his final message of peace. Perhaps never before in our time has a human word —the word of a master, a leader, a prophet, a pope—rung out so loudly and won such affection throughout the whole world." Crowds continued to gather in St. Peter's Square, praying and weeping, waiting and praying. In the middle of the night passing into June 3, Pope John awoke and said twice with great emphasis, "Lord, you know that I love you." These were his last distinct words. He was preparing to die. The crowd in St. Peter's, as if under a spell, grew larger yet. The world media was there within the vigil. Everyone present was swept up in the power of this gentle man from Bergamo, this funny and kind man, this noble churchman drawn from farmers.

On June 3, a large outdoor Mass began in the piazza at 5:00 PM as crowds thronged to pray—people of every faith on earth, people who felt that they had known this man personally. Their loss was personal, not ecclesial. In John they had an advocate. If you were poor, he took your part. If you were outside the Church, he reminded you how much the Church loved you. If you were a nonbeliever, he offered you his friendship. If you were rejected, he took you in.

The crowd in the piazza had grown quiet and prayerful as Cardinal Traglia presided at Mass. It seemed as though two sacrifices were being enacted simultaneously: that of John, the servant of the servants of God, alongside that of the altar.

At Pope John's bedside were farmers and cardinals: the story of his life. Members of his family were present, along with Monsignor Capovilla, his doctors, and the nuns from Bergamo who had been his housekeepers. At 7:45 the Mass being celebrated in St. Peter's Square came to an end with the audible *Ite Missa Est* ("you may go," or "you are sent"). Everyone in the now-silent bedchamber of the dying man could hear those words through the open June window of the Vatican. Pope John gave a last faint rattle. His breathing became very weak, then stopped completely. It was 7:49 PM, June 3, 1963. Pope John XXIII was dead.

In the Mass as it was celebrated in that era, the "Last Gospel" (the prologue of the Gospel of John) was proclaimed after the final blessing. Cardinal Traglia proclaimed it in Latin, including the words *Fuit homo missus a Deo, cui nomen erat Joannes*: "There was a man sent from God whose name was John." Heaven and earth seemed to come together to welcome Pope John home.

Spiritual Exercise

A PRAYER OF GRATITUDE

Step One » *Prepare to pray with a few moments of quiet.*
Now, in your own words, compose a prayerful letter to Saint
John XXIII. In my own prayer with Pope John, I call him by his
Italian name, Papa Giovanni. It's an intimate name, one that
helps me sense his presence among us. We have much to tell
him and much more to learn from him. This letter will help you
begin to capture those lessons. It is also a chance to ask him to
be present on your behalf to the Lord. Here is my own letter to
him; I happen to be writing this on the anniversary of both his
birthday and his baptism, November 25, 2013.

Dear Papa Giovanni,
Thank you for the great sense of hope and happiness
which you have brought to the Church. Thank you for
your encyclicals and the Second Vatican Council, of
course. May they lead us to peace and to a renewed
Church. I am so grateful that you trusted that "flash of
heavenly light" and opened the windows of the Church
to let in the fresh air we are still breathing today.

But beyond all that, thank you for making your own
ordinary life so holy. Like me, you came from farm
stock, hardworking and faithful. Your desire for holiness has taught me to desire it, too. In your humility and
poverty, you shared our own lives. Whether we lived
in the slums, prisons, and orphanages of Rome or the
citadels of power, you gave us your heart. You gave your
heart to all the people of the world, and you helped us
all experience the mystery of God, the mystery of divine

love, in our very midst. You lit the eternal light once again, not only for Catholics, but for all men and women of good will, even for those who could see only darkness and despair until they heard your call.

Thank you for speaking in our language. You spoke, I know, in Latin or Italian, but we all understood you clearly in our own tongue. This was the new Pentecost. I, too, have heard you, Papa Giovanni, and I wish to spend my life helping others also understand. Thank you for the humor and joy, for the reason to hope, and for the example of your holy death.

You are in heaven now. Speak a word of comfort to Margaret and Herman, my dear parents, who are with you. Greet my friend and teacher, good Bishop Ray Lucker. Join the party with them all and raise a toast to us. Speak a word to the Lord on my behalf. Ask for strength for my work and for courage to continue my journey to holiness. And when the time comes for me to join you there, may Mary and the angels lead me to your side where we will enjoy the comfort of God's eternal peace. Amen.

Step Two » *Write.*

With pencil and paper now, write a letter yourself to this gentle, loving man who is our friend.

PRINCIPLES FOR A HOLY LIFE

In many Italian families, there exists a recipe for pasta sauce that is kept as a family secret. No one would ever whisper the "secrets of the sauce" to anyone outside the family. It might be fennel, or a certain type of garlic, or how the tomatoes are prepared—but it remains a secret. Pope John also had some "secrets of his sauce." You might say these secrets were the magic that allowed him to accomplish so much in such a short time. They are the principles on which he based his actions, thinking, prayer, and decisions. Taken together, the "secrets of his sauce" form a way of being present to God, to others, and even to himself. These ways of being can teach us all some lessons.

1. Keep Christ before you.
First and foremost, on his deathbed, Pope John revealed his most important secret:

I keep before me at all times

93

the crucifix;
it is the secret of my ministry
and a summary of my time as pope.
Those open arms of Christ there,
    they have been what I wanted for the Church,
    to open our arms to all.
These arms remind us that Christ died for all.
    When I say "died for all"
    I mean really and truly everyone on earth,
        excluding no one from his love and forgiveness.

2. Search for everyday holiness.

Pope John spent his life seeking everyday holiness. This simple desire was a great secret of his success. By his seeking only holiness, everything else fell into place, and negative thoughts, criticisms against him, or selfishness fell away from him. It isn't that he was sinless; he knew well enough his own sins and confessed them weekly. It is rather that everyday holiness gave him freedom and saved him from himself. On retreat in 1961, he wrote about this in his own journal.

Everyone calls me by the title "Holy Father."
    Well, then, holy I must be!
I am very far away from actually being holy enough, however.
    Yet, it is what I desire above all.
    I am determined that I will move in that direction.
Such holiness means I must be willing
    to be opposed and even humiliated,
    whether my opponents are right or wrong.
It means I must respond to the needs of the Church,
    to put myself at the service of others.
It means I must be aware that I am only an earthen vessel,

that I am "nothing,"
in order to let the Lord shine through me.
It leads me to be grateful to others,
  to love sincerely,
    to be calm in the face of the storm,
    to be gentle in my treatment of others,
    and to work unceasingly in love.
This is all there is.

3. Trust that God is leading you.

Pope John trusted that God would lead him, if only he could allow God to do so. His motto summed it up: "Obedience and Peace." Speaking to a group of pilgrims from Venice who had come to see him in Rome in March 1959, he told them:

If you wish to know the secret of my life,
  it is simple.
Do not look beyond this for any deeper explanation.
  I have kept before me
  the words of St. Gregory Nazianzen:
"Not our will but the will of God is our peace."

Later that same year, he wrote in his journal that he was grateful that God had given him a temperament that kept him from feeling anxious or from worrying over complex solutions to simple challenges. He wrote, in summary:

My secret is that I believe I must live in obedience
  regarding everything in my life and the Church.
This attitude of trusting where God is leading me,
  even though I know I am a sinner,
  gives me great strength and daring,

in a simple sort of way,
>which leads others to Christ by example.
Because my actions flow from God's own directives,
>they are received with respect by most people.
I am humbled by this and I pray:
>Lord, I am indeed not worthy.
>Be my strength now and always,
>>be the source of my happiness.
>You are my God! You are my mercy!

4. Be strong, but be humble.

Pope John was humble and gracious toward all. He loved people more than power, as Yves Congar once remarked. He was widely loved by Catholics but also by people of all faiths or even of no faith whatsoever. He was open to allowing the Spirit to move him in surprising ways. On retreat in the Vatican in 1959, following an Ignatian inspiration, he made notes in his journal that read like this, in summary:

The way in which people welcome me
>and the affection that so many people show me,
>always comes as a great surprise!
The secret of my success in this area
>is that I do not search into things
>that are above my ability
>>and I am quite content
>>>to be meek and humble.
Meekness and humility put other people at ease
>and make me gracious in meeting them,
>>in talking together,
>>and in dealing with people in general.
This is so because if one is humble,

what does he have to lose in showing love?
Above all, I am always ready
   for the Lord's surprise moves.
You never know what happiness or pain
   you may be called on to bear.

5. *Grow and change constantly.*

Pope John knew deeply that to remain strong in God's grace, we must change and grow constantly. There are many examples of this in his life, but one stands out. From his earliest days in the seminary, and even before that in his home life, he wanted to follow God and learn to be holy. He set himself on a pathway that he believed would take him there. The year was 1903, and he was in the seminary. Here's what he wrote in his journal:

Ever since I finished the Spiritual Exercises
   (of St. Ignatius)
   I feel the need to start over
   on my spiritual journey.
Much as I hate to admit this
   I am still a poor sinner:
      I am not loyal enough;
      I'm proud beyond belief;
      I'm not thinking clearly;
      My manners are poor;
      And I feel worthless.
Oh Jesus, have mercy on me!

Two weeks later, having reflected on his plans to grow in holiness, he realized he needed to make some changes, so he wrote:

Now that I've had some actual experience in life,

I can plainly see that the concept of holiness
which I had formed for myself
and which I followed carefully
was mistaken.
Every time I failed to live a holy life
I called to mind some saint
whom I admire and wish to imitate
down to the smallest detail.
A painter may wish to make an exact copy of a Raphael,
for instance.
Likewise, I used to say to myself
that I wished to be an exact copy of some saint:
he would have done that or this;
he would not have thought such and so.
I was never able to live up to these demands
and I worried myself about it terribly.
Now I can see that the method was wrong.

From the saints I must take their attitude,
their love of Christ,
their kind actions and self-giving.
I am not St. Aloysius
and I can never be.
I must not seek holiness his way;
I must seek it as I am called
in my own particular way.
I cannot become a dry, lifeless reproduction
of someone else
but I must be my own self.
God desires only that we follow the examples of the saints,
not that we become them.

6. Don't let anyone stop you!

Pope John seemed to have an inborn optimism about all matters, within the Church and outside it. This optimism emerged from a youthful and playful presence with all those who came into contact with him. To longtime Vatican insiders, this was considered a fault. But to many around the world who had had so little personal contact with the papacy in the past 400 years, this new youthful vigor, especially in an eighty-year-old man, opened both doors and hearts. He "carried on" with Protestants, Jews, unbelievers, communists, the Eastern churches, and many others heretofore unwelcome at the Vatican. He behaved as though we had nothing to fear from anyone and as though God might choose anyone to deliver God's message to us.

He likewise looked to the youthful years of the Church, those first centuries when it was animated more fervently by the spirit of Jesus. He never fell victim to fear, but only continued to believe that God in our age was preparing to do great work, as great as that done during those earliest years of the Christian community.

This showed itself most prominently in his dealings with the staff of the Curia while preparations were underway for the Council. There, in ways unchanged since the sixteenth century, officials protected age-old ways of understanding the Church and their roles in it. Pope John worked patiently but insistently to add a youthfulness of spirit to their view. He dreamed of a "new springtime" for the Church. Despite the resistance of these Vatican insiders, Pope John persisted.

One day, for example, shortly after he had announced his intention to hold Vatican II, a faithful prelate of the Curia, thinking it might require ten to twenty years of preparation to get Vatican II ready, told him, "It's absolutely impossible to open the Council in 1963."

"Fine," Pope John replied, "we'll open it in 1962 then!"

7. Always look forward with hope.

Pope John did not look back, and neither should we. He was a great leader in the Church, but now the time has come to go forward with vigor and undertake the work that is given to us. As he himself said of the saints, our task is not to become them, but to be ourselves in possession of their faith and hope. Here, in closing, is a summary of Pope John's ideas about this.

When he was my age,
    my mentor and friend Bishop Radini
    was dying.
Sometimes when I remember that,
    I am tempted to think of myself as an old man.
I must resist this thinking.
    Despite how old I might look
    inside I want to keep a youthfulness of spirit,
        a modernity of mind.
I think this youthfulness pleases God;
    it's a good example to others
    and it's good for me, too.
After all, it's my duty to fill others
    with joy and optimism.
I am thankful to God that I prefer to look forward
    rather than backward.
I carry with me wonderful memories of old friends
    but instead of dwelling in "what was"
    I look forward to the glory of "what will be."
As we say good bye to our dear family and friends
        throughout life,
    we weep and wave goodbye.

But these very same people are the ones
    waiting at the dock to welcome us
    when we arrive where they have gone.

What might we expect to have learned from Saint John XXIII? Did we learn profound theological insights? Did we learn deep secrets about the mystery of God? Eternal truths? All of these, yes, perhaps. But the real spiritual wisdom of Saint John XXIII is more than that. We learned how to live with gusto, how to love tenderly, how to laugh, and how to die in peace.

Notes and Credits

In the preparation of this manuscript, one of my most reliable and important sources was written by Pope John XXIII himself and is the well-known *Journal of a Soul* (Trans by Dorothy White. New York: McGraw Hill, 1965). This is an amazing record of the spiritual journey of Angelo Roncalli from his early years in Sotto il Monte where he was born to the papal apartment in which he died.

Anyone writing about Pope John XXIII is indebted to Peter Hebblethwaite. His two major books in English on this pope are the landmark biographies from which so many have drawn inspiration and information. First is his 1985 *Pope John XXIII: Shepherd of the Modern World* (Doubleday) which is the definitive biography of John XXIII. He followed that in 1994 with *John XXIII: Pope of the Council* (Harpercollins/STL) and later, *John XXIII: Pope of the Century* (Continuum), published in 2005.

I also found Thomas Cahill's 2002 *Pope John XXIII* (Penguin Life Series: Penguin Books) very helpful. Cahill sets the papacy of John XXIII in the context of Church history, showing clearly how Pope John opened the windows of the Church to the modern world.

Another wonderful resource for me was also written by Pope

John XXIII himself and is published under the title *Prayers and Devotions from Pope John XXIII* (Ed. John P. Donnelly. Trans. Dorothy White. New York: Grosset & Dunlap, 1967).

Ernesto Balducci is the author of another key resource entitled *John: "The Transitional Pope"* (Trans by Dorothy White. New York and London: McGraw Hill and Burns and Oates, 1965). This is a terrific personal record of Balducci's experience of Pope John during his life, death, and legacy periods. I have read and reread this book over the years many times.

There are many small collections of stories and sayings about Pope John but one I especially like is from Kurt Klinger who collected a very representative group of them in *A Pope Laughs: Stories of John XXIII* (Trans. Sally McDevitt Cunneen. New York: Holt, Reinhart and Winston, 1963).

Another such collection was collected by Henri Fesquet in *Wit and Wisdom of Good Pope John* (Trans. Salvator Attanasio. New York: P.J. Kenedy & Sons, 1964).

And yet another is from Alden Hatch who published them under the title *A Man Named John* (New York: Hawthorn Books, 1963).

In terms of Pope John's letters, discourses, and speeches, there is the essential *The Encyclicals and Other Messages of John XXIII* (Washington, DC: TPS Press, 1964). In it, among other important messages of Pope John, I found *Thoughts for the Council's Recess,* which was published and sent to all the bishops of the world in January 1963. Pope John knew he was sick when he wrote this, but he could not have known he would die just five months later.

That great story about Pope John's sculptor, Giacomo Manzu, came from a book written specifically about him. It is one of my favorite books on Pope John because it shows him "behind the scenes" of Vatican protocol. It was written by Curtis Bill Pepper with Giacomo Manzu and is published under the title *An Artist and the Pope* (New York: Madison Square Press, 1968).

When I summarized sections from the Council documents I relied on *Vatican Council II: The Basic Sixteen Documents*, by Austin Flannery, OP © 1996 (Costello Publishing Company, Inc). And when I quoted Scripture, I used *The Message: The Bible in Contemporary Language (Catholic/Ecumenical edition)*, © 2013 (Chicago, IL: ACTA Publications).

Conclusion

I just can't resist sharing one last idea from Pope John, one that came from his own journal. Here's a summary of what he wrote:

Yesterday my learned teacher in church history
  gave us excellent advice,
    particularly useful to me: "Read little, little but well."
What he said about reading seems correct to me
  so I plan to apply it to everything else:
    little but well.

In the preparation of this account of the spiritual wisdom of this great saint, I've tried to provide you with a little, well-chosen material. I hope this "little but well" collection of the prayers, advice, journal entries, speeches, and personal encounters of Pope John inspires you to your own sainthood.

More resources on Saint John XXIII

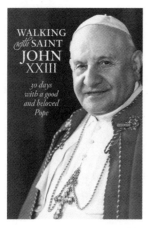

32 PAGES | $1.95 | 9781627850056

WALKING WITH SAINT JOHN XXIII
30 Days with a Good and Beloved Pope

In this little booklet, we invite you to walk with Saint John XXIII for thirty days, reflecting on his teachings—with related Scripture passages, prayers, and practices—all meant to help you follow in his footsteps. This is a wonderful spiritual guide for celebrating "Good Pope John," one of our Church's newest saints!

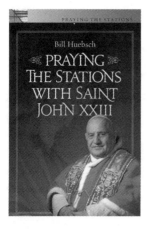

32 PAGES | $1.95 | 9781627850049

PRAYING THE STATIONS WITH SAINT JOHN XXIII
Bill Huebsch

Based on extensive scholarship and prayerful study, Bill Huebsch has faithfully adapted the fourteen Stations of the Cross to the message and teaching of John XXIII. Each combines the traditional Station prayer with a Psalm response and reflection about John's life that resonates in our modern world.

1-800-321-0411
WWW.23RDPUBLICATIONS.COM

TWENTY THIRD 23rd
PUBLICATIONS